Six Essays in
Comparative Sociology

Six Essays in
Comparative Sociology

ANDRÉ BÉTEILLE

DELHI
OXFORD UNIVERSITY PRESS
LONDON NEW YORK
1974

Oxford University Press, Ely House, London W.1.
GLASGOW NEW YORK TORONTO MELBOURNE WELLINGTON
CAPE TOWN IBADAN NAIROBI DAR ES SALAAM LUSAKA ADDIS ABABA
DELHI BOMBAY CALCUTTA MADRAS KARACHI LAHORE DACCA
KUALA LUMPUR SINGAPORE HONG KONG TOKYO
2/11 Ansari Road, Daryaganj, Delhi 6

André BÉTEILLE 1934

Printed in India by P. K. Ghosh at Eastend Printers, 3 Dr Suresh
Sarkar Road, Calcutta 14 and published by John Brown,
Oxford University Press, 2/11 Ansari Road, Daryaganj, Delhi 6

TO MY FATHER

Preface

In September 1972 I was invited by the University Grants Commission to deliver the National Lectures in Sociology for 1972-73. This book is an outcome of that invitation.

My initial plan was to write a set of three lectures and to deliver them at three universities. After I had written the third lecture—in January 1973—I felt I needed to write three more in order to reveal more clearly the connexions among the first three and to relate the whole effort to the concerns of sociology in contemporary India. The first three essays were delivered as lectures at Chandigarh, Aligarh and Lucknow. The fourth and fifth were never really delivered as lectures. The sixth is based on a lecture that I have given from time to time to students in the Department of Sociology at the University of Delhi.

The first essay looks backward; the last, I hope, is forward looking. I doubt if in the years to come many serious students of society in India will worry greatly about the distinction between sociology and social anthropology except as a problem in academic administration or academic politics. But I do believe that Indian sociologists must increasingly come to terms with Marxists who are also students of society but with a different perspective. So far they have behaved towards each other rather like half-brothers; each has pretended, at least in public, to be more or less unaware of the other's existence. As I see it, there are certain fundamental differences between Marxism and academic sociology which it will be very hard to resolve; but there is also much common ground between the two. Sociology has no doctrine to defend, hence sociologists need have little fear of losing their faith by being exposed to Marxism.

This is my second exercise in comparative sociology; the first was a selection of readings on social inequality which I edited for Penguin Books. Indian sociologists have by and large fought shy of doing comparative sociology, but have provided raw materials to others interested in pursuing cross-cultural studies.

There are special reasons why Indians have confined themselves mainly to the study of their own society. They have far fewer resources for studying other societies and cultures than have American or European scholars. Yet I believe it to be not only possible but also fruitful for Indians to work in the framework of comparative sociology while keeping India at the centre of their minds. In contributing to comparative sociology, Indians will have to look increasingly to neighbouring countries like China, Pakistan and Bangladesh.

I am grateful to many people for their stimulation in the preparation of these essays, and especially to Jit Uberoi from whom I have learnt much in the course of our close and somewhat contentious association. I was treated with much kindness at the three universities which I visited for delivering the National Lectures. My special thanks are due to Professor V. S. D'Souza, his colleagues and students at the Department of Sociology, Panjab University; to Professor R. N. Saksena, his colleagues and students at the Department of Sociology, Aligarh Muslim University; and to Dr. K. S. Mathur, his colleagues and students at the Department of Anthropology, Lucknow University.

Finally, I would like to thank the University Grants Commission for inviting me to deliver the first series of National Lectures in Sociology—an undeserved honour which I gratefully acknowledge.

Contents

1

Sociology and Social Anthropology

It is useful to examine the relationship between sociology and social anthropology as it has taken shape during the last few decades in order to see more clearly the work being done by scholars in these fields in India today. Most textbooks devote a few paragraphs to the topic, but the discussion is generally presented in somewhat abstract, and even ideal, terms. A purely formal discussion of the subject will not be very useful any longer: a discussion at this stage will serve a purpose only if it creates a deeper awareness of the work in which we are actually engaged.

Contrary to what they say, academics are much preoccupied with labels. But if our discussion is to be fruitful we must look into the reality that lies behind the labels. Are the investigations made by sociologists and social anthropologists basically similar or are they basically different? If they are basically similar, then why divide the investigators into two categories and draw an artificial line between them? If they are basically different, then why not maintain the distinction between them consistently and why are people, particularly in India, continually changing roles, appearing now as sociologists and again as social anthropologists? We should take a critical look at the prevailing division of work among students of human society and culture.

One might feel that ideally this division of work ought to be the same throughout the world; but we know that in reality this is not the case. The relationship between sociology and social anthropology is not the same in France as in Britain, and the difference was greater sixty years ago. Anglophone countries have, on the whole, maintained a distinction between the two, and this distinction was at its sharpest in the period between the two World Wars. The division of labour between sociology and social anthropology emerged in Britain or the United States under specific historical conditions, and was then transmitted to other countries where conditions were different. There is no ground to believe that what appeared reasonable and appropriate under certain conditions will always appear to be so.

A proper division of work among students of human society can be established only on the basis of their ultimate academic objectives and their actual academic concerns. But in dealing with the relationship between sociology and social anthropology we are faced not only with academic distinctions but also with administrative divisions. In the administrative sense this relationship is already established when a university or a research institution decides to regard the two as the same or as different. It is beyond the scope of the present discussion to review the administrative organization of the social sciences in India. But clearly, the division of labour among scholars should be governed ultimately by academic and not by administrative considerations.

In India sociology and social anthropology as academic disciplines are of relatively recent growth. The first university departments were started at Bombay and Calcutta a little over fifty years ago, but the real growth in their organization began only after Independence. This is in a sense fortunate for it means that the pattern of administrative organization that has emerged has barely had time to acquire a rigid form. This makes it particularly appropriate to examine now the rationale of the division of labour that is taking shape.

In examining the relationship between sociology and social anthropology we must begin by recognizing that there is no single conception of either. We must not forget that as recently as thirty years ago anthropologists were sharply divided about their basic frame of reference even within the Anglo-American tradition. British anthropologists, following largely the lead of Radcliffe-Brown, regarded social structure as their basic field of interest, while Americans were more in favour of the study of culture.[1] While this particular debate

[1] For the British point of view see R. Firth, 'Contemporary British Social Anthropology', *American Anthropologist*, Vol. 53, pp. 474–90, 1951; for the American point of view see G. P. Murdock, 'British Social Anthropology', *American Anthropologist*, Vol. 53, pp. 465–73, 1951.

has died down—and in retrospect appears to have been rather fruitless —other differences may still be observed.

The European way of looking at the subject has been somewhat different again. In Europe the term anthropology has generally been used in a restricted sense to refer only to physical anthropology, whereas what the British and the Americans referred to as social and cultural anthropology was broadly described as ethnology. As Radcliffe-Brown pointed out many years ago, social anthropology and ethnology did not have identical orientations.[2]

It is necessary to point out that we are dealing here with differences not only in labels but also in contents. Those who described their work as ethnology or as cultural anthropology felt justified in investigating both material and non-material culture. In Britain, on the other hand, the change from the phase of ethnology to that of social anthropology was accompanied by a quiet withdrawal of interest from the study of material culture. Now, it does make a difference whether or not we consider the study of the material culture of a people as essential to an understanding of their social institutions.

In turning to sociology in the restricted sense, we are struck no less by the different ways in which sociologists have conceived their subject. About forty years ago Karl Mannheim wrote two essays, one on American sociology and the other on German sociology, in which he contrasted the empiricism of the former with the philosophical preoccupations of the latter.[3] On the whole, the Anglo-Saxons have a different approach to sociology from the Europeans, and when they feel particularly ill at ease with European sociology, they tend to characterize it as social philosophy, or just philosophy.

To add to this, we now have Soviet sociology which defines itself in opposition to 'bourgeois sociology'.[4] The history of sociology in the Soviet Union is in itself a subject which calls for separate treatment. Although it had its origins at the turn of the century, it did not find a fertile field for development in Russia after the Revolution. In its present form it is of relatively recent origin—going back not more

[2] A. R. Radcliffe-Brown, 'The Methods of Ethnology and Social Anthropology' in M. N. Srinivas (ed.), *Method in Social Anthropology, Selected Essays by A. R. Radcliffe-Brown*, Asia, 1960.

[3] Karl Mannheim, 'American Sociology' and 'German Sociology (1917–1933)' in *Essays in Sociology and Social Psychology*, Routledge and Kegan Paul, 1953.

[4] For a representative example see G. Osipov, *Sociology*, Progress Publishers, 1969.

than twenty years—and it is perhaps too early to say what shape it will eventually acquire.

So much diversity in the conception of what is sociology and what is social anthropology may be a sign of vitality, but it can also become a source of confusion. If one wishes to assert the fundamental unity of the two subjects, a particular conception of sociology can be chosen and it can be shown to be the same as the prevailing conception of social anthropology. But by choosing another conception of sociology someone else can highlight not the similarities between the two subjects but their differences. Which conception of sociology or of social anthropology one prefers will in turn depend on how the relationship between the two is viewed.

This brings us to a consideration of the difference between principle and practice, between what people believe or declare to be their ultimate objective and what they actually do. There is no reason to think that in the social sciences, any more than in other spheres of social life, there will be perfect correspondence between the two.

It might happen that two sets of people define their ultimate objectives in very different terms, but in actual practice engage in much the same kind of work. Thus, in spite of their very different basic orientations, there might be much in common between Soviet and American sociologists in the work they actually do. On the other hand—and this is what concerns us more—people might define their broad objectives in the same terms but actually work in very different ways. I would argue that sociology and social anthropology have similar or even identical aims, and yet sociologists and social anthropologists have often done very different kinds of work.

The comparative study of social interaction and of social institutions became fairly well-established in Europe and America by the beginning of the present century. The stimulus to this kind of study was provided by the growing awareness that the methods of science could be properly applied to the study of social facts. Social life was seen to have patterns, and the exploration of these patterns became the principal concern of a number of scholars who were initially recruited from a variety of disciplines.

There were two aspects of these studies which gave them a distinctive character from the very beginning, and which continue to be their defining features even today. The first is a general sense of the interrelatedness of the different institutions of a society. Some scholars have emphasized some institutions more than others, but they have all sought to view society as a system, however loosely integrated. The second is the application, in some form or other, of what I would call the comparative method. Again, some scholars have sought to make broader generalizations than others, but they have all acknowledged the utility of comparing institutions of various societies in order to reveal their similarities and differences.

Now if we define sociology in this way, we will see at once that it can serve equally well for a definition of social anthropology. This indeed was the argument of Radcliffe-Brown who maintained that social anthropology was the same as comparative sociology. As is well known, Radcliffe-Brown enjoyed great prestige among social anthropologists in the English-speaking countries, and one of his pupils, W. Lloyd Warner, occupied a pre-eminent position among American sociologists in the thirties and forties. But despite the logic of Radcliffe-Brown's argument, sociologists and social anthropologists remained for the most part divided in their work in countries such as Britain, the United States, Australia and Canada.

If we are to understand why Radcliffe-Brown's logic made so little headway against established habits, we must find out how these habits came to be established. Sociology and social anthropology had both begun by asking general questions about the nature and origins of human society as a whole. They became scientific disciplines only when they began to make empirical investigations into particular societies. Now the types of societies social anthropologists and sociologists chose to study in detail were from the start very different from each other. Thus, it is an irony that in Britain and America the very process that transferred the study of society from the plane of philosophical speculation to that of scientific investigation also led to an increasing divergence between sociology and social anthropology.

Despite Radcliffe-Brown's admonitions, in Britain social anthropology became in effect the study of primitive, pre-literate or tribal societies in the colonies instead of developing into comparative sociology in the full sense of the term. Radcliffe-Brown's own empirical investigations were made among the Andaman Islanders and the Australian aborigines, and his comparisons were comparisons of the institutions of tribal societies. Malinowski did not go even so far as that; his writings were based almost wholly on his fieldwork in the Trobriand Islands.

Malinowski's pupils worked mainly in Africa where they investigated the institutions of a variety of tribal societies. These investigations brought out in a vivid way the manifold interrelations among the different institutions of particular societies, and in this way contributed much to the understanding of the basic principles of social life. There were also comparative studies of politics, kinship and cosmology among African tribes. These detailed studies of tribal life—both particular and general—besides contributing to theory, were also of some practical value to colonial administrators.

George Homans pointed out some years ago, with some exaggeration, that students of human society in Britain seemed to believe that the only societies requiring scientific study were those of the native tribes, but never their own.[5] It was for this reason, he said, that Britain had produced outstanding anthropologists but no sociologist. While this might not be altogether fair, it certainly drew attention to the fact that in Britain a sociologist would be a person who studied British society or societies of the British kind; and in general he would be a very different person from one who studied native societies.

Colonial rule inevitably projects the view that the institutions and customs of the ruling country are fundamentally different from those of the colonies. The distinction between those who study their own society and those who study other cultures is one reflection of this view. It is no accident that it reached its peak at the height of the colonial regime. With the end of this regime, sociologists and social anthropologists are beginning to come closer to each other in Britain.

Colonial rule is not the only condition which highlights the differences between societies. In the United States this condition was provided primarily by the co-existence of two very different kinds of social and cultural systems within the same country. No contrast could be sharper than the one between the complex, technologically-advanced and aggressive civilization of the industrial cities and the pre-literate, technologically-backward and moribund culture of the tribal reservations. It is out of this contrast that the distinction was born in the United States between sociology and social or cultural anthropology.

The great American anthropologists of the first half of the twentieth century—Boas, Kroeber, Lowie—all concentrated on the study of American Indian tribes. These tribes were for the most part isolated in reservations where they lived under special conditions. These conditions differed not only from those in the industrial cities but

[5] G. C. Homans, 'Giving a Dog a Bad Name' in G. C. Homans, *Sentiments and Activities*, Routledge and Kegan Paul, 1962.

also from the conditions under which the American Indians had lived before the Europeans came. The reason why American anthropologists at first concentrated on the study of culture traits is that the people they studied had for the most part ceased to have ongoing social systems of the kind which could be observed by British social anthropologists in Africa.[6]

The ongoing social systems studied by the Americans were those which were taking shape in the rapidly expanding industrial cities. Americans have not shown the kind of inhibition about examining their own society that Homans says he found among the British. On the contrary, they have produced a larger volume of empirical investigations than has been produced by sociologists in any other part of the world. Further, until recently American sociologists have been preoccupied with the study of their own society to the virtual exclusion of all other societies.

The city has loomed large in the investigations of American sociologists. As is well known, the strength of American sociology—like that of British social anthropology—has been its grounding in empirical research. The problems of work and management in factory and office, of leisure and recreation in the home and neighbourhood, the different sectors of the city and their socio-economic characteristics—it is the study of these that has given to American sociology its distinctive shape. By contrast rural sociology has always been a low-priority and low-prestige subject in the United States.

Primitive and civilized societies came to be studied by different sets of scholars on the view that they were very different from each other. These differences were real and not imaginary, although they were probably exaggerated by the manner in which the study of social life came to be organized. When all societies are studied within the framework of a single discipline one is likely to regard them as variants of the same basic pattern. When their study becomes divided between separate disciplines, one is more likely to regard them as representing basically different patterns.

If social anthropologists have paid much attention to the study of kinship systems, it is because these systems *are* so much more conspicuous and pervasive in tribal as opposed to industrial societies. Where, as among the Australian aborigines, the entire community can

[6] A similar point has been made by Max Gluckman, *Politics, Law and Ritual in Tribal Societies*, Basil Blackwell, 1965, pp. 33–4.

2

be represented on a single genealogy, the study of genealogies and the values attached to genealogical ties naturally becomes important.

Again, when four separate terms are used for describing cousins, this naturally becomes a subject of interest to the investigator in whose own society only a single term is used. The collection and analysis of kinship terms by the genealogical method has been since the time of Rivers an essential part of the training of every anthropologist. By contrast, the study of kinship and marraige—as distinct from family relations—has been of little concern among sociologists, particularly in the United States. When Homans embarked on a study of pre-ferential kin marriage, he felt he was playing the role of an anthro-pologist, which was something unusual in an American sociologist.[7]

What the study of kinship was to anthropology, the study of social class or stratification was to sociology. Here also the approach to the problem differed somewhat between European and American socio-logists. The former were more concerned with the study of class in the Marxian sense; the concerns of the latter centred more generally around prestige and social ranking. The anthropologist showed little interest in these problems because the tribal societies he studied did not generally have either clearly graded strata or mutually opposed classes.

Studies of kinship on the one hand and of stratification on the other have generated highly specialized bodies of literature, each having its own methodology, its own array of concepts and its own technical vocabulary. This difference is clearly reflected in the contents of pro-fessional journals, particularly in America. Not many sociologists today feel they have the competence to contribute to or even follow the current discussions in the field of kinship theory; similarly, most anthropologists would be baffled by the subtleties of the techniques being developed for the study of social stratification. This is in a way unfortunate because the problems of kinship and of social inequality are of general if not universal significance to students of human society.

Tribal and industrial societies represent two extremes, whether we view them on an evolutionary scale or simply arrange them according to size and complexity of structure. In the West anthropologists have been particularly attracted to the most primitive or elementary forms, and sociologists to the most advanced or complex forms of human society. If either or both had chosen to work on middle ground, the

[7] G. C Homans, 'Introduction', op. cit.

differences we see between them might not have emerged. As we have remarked, historical factors played an important part in leading them to choose societies whose differences were more manifest than their similarities.

Given this fundamental difference in the point of departure for empirical inquiries, other differences were bound to develop. But these are of secondary importance. We have already observed that there are differences in the institutional areas typically emphasized by sociologists and social anthropologists, but these in themselves are not what matter. When someone studies kinship and marriage in a New York suburb he can claim to be a sociologist; but when he studies status and rank among the Kwakiutl Indians he will be regarded as an anthropologist. In America—and to some extent also in Britain—what really counts is the kind of society one investigates, not which aspect of it one analyses.

Again, while sociologists and social anthropologists in Britain and America tend to use different sets of concepts, it would be a mistake to regard this as the basic source of their difference. Differences in the conceptual apparatus became more pronounced the more definitely scholars began to concentrate on empirical studies of opposite kinds of society. And in spite of this, basic concepts such as 'structure', 'function', 'status', 'role', 'conflict', 'change' and 'evolution' continue to be used in much the same way by sociologists and social anthropologists.

Much has been made of the differences in method used by students of the two varieties of human society. However, firstly, these differences are not as large as they are often made to appear. Secondly, no field of scientific inquiry can be defined by its method. What is of fundamental importance is the problem; it is the problem of study which should determine the method to be used. I would go further and distinguish between approach, method and technique, and say that sociology and social anthropology have the same approach to the study of social life, that their methods are similar, but that they have developed different techniques of investigation and analysis.

The contrast between anthropology and sociology is often drawn in terms of the opposition between the methods of intensive fieldwork and of survey research. This way of making a contrast appears to be empirically false and logically untenable. No sociologist interested in the study of real societies would like to deny himself the possibility of doing intensive fieldwork; no anthropologist would like to exclude in principle the possibility of doing survey research.

Intensive fieldwork is particularly suited to the requirements of studying pre-literate tribal societies. A Western scholar who wishes to collect data on tribal life has to travel a great distance to make his observations. If an Englishman, he has to leave his country and travel to Africa or Melanesia or Australia. If an American, he has to travel at least from his urban home to a reservation. This itself is a major investment, and one who makes it would naturally like to stay in the field long enough to be able to get a reasonable return on it. Those who have seen British anthropologists preparing to set out for field-work in Africa can understand why they seek to remain in the field for at least a year.

There are other reasons why the anthropologist needs to spend a long time in the field. If he is to collect reliable data he must learn the local language; the sociologist already knows this, since in Britain and America he usually studies his own society. The anthropologist not only must learn a new language but has also to make himself familiar with new categories of thought. In this way he collects his data and ensures that they are reliable and meaningful. All this makes it essential for him to proceed with patience and care. Other techniques of investigation can be applied only after the anthropologist has got his bearings straight through the method of intensive fieldwork.

In Britain and America sociologists study the working of institutions with whose basic nature they are to some extent already familiar. Hence they can afford to miss the preliminary step of getting acquainted with an unfamiliar culture. But clearly, this is only a matter of degree. In a complex industrial society there are many compartments, and when a sociologist seeks to probe into one which is very different from those in which he has grown up, he too must start with intensive fieldwork. William Foote Whyte has described how the world of an American slum was so different from his own middle class environment that in order to study it he was compelled to use the method of intensive fieldwork.[8]

These considerations have led some to reformulate the distinction between anthropology and sociology in slightly different terms. It has been said that anthropology is the study of 'other cultures', implying that sociology is basically the study of one's own society and

[8] William F. Whyte, *Street Corner Society*, University of Chicago Press, 1955, Appendix.

culture. Lévi-Strauss has emphasized the differences of perspective in the study of one's own as opposed to alien institutions.[9]

But this way of making a distinction can lead only to confusion. For if applied consistently, what anthropology is to an American will be sociology to an Indian, and what sociology is to an American will be anthropology to an Indian. The distinction will work only so long as all societies, Western and non-Western, are studied only by Western scholars. It becomes meaningless when scholars from all over the world begin to study their own as well as other societies.

If the arrangement of work among students of society in Britain and America is a response to a particular set of conditions, then we can expect a different arrangement in countries where the conditions are different or are perceived differently. However, there are many complicating factors. Habits of work among scholars might persist even when the conditions which gave rise to them have changed. Further, habits of work which originate in one country might be transmitted to another even though they are quite inappropriate to the conditions there.

It would be wrong to suggest that colonialism necessarily creates a dichotomy between anthropology and sociology, as happened to a large extent in Britain. If we turn to France which also had a colonial empire we will find a somewhat different pattern of relationship between students of primitive and of civilized societies. This relationship has changed between the end of the last century and the present time. If in France at a certain stage the study of all types of human societies became part of the same intellectual endeavour, this probably happened despite the colonial reality which divided the world into two. But the reality soon made its presence felt, so that in France perhaps even more than in Britain the study of primitive and civilized societies are now two different things.

Radcliffe-Brown's idea referred to earlier, that there can be only one science of comparative sociology embracing the study of all human societies, did not in fact originate with him, but with his distinguished French predecessor, Émile Durkheim. Durkheim occupies a unique position in the history of sociological thought. He is regarded as a founding father equally by sociologists and by social anthropologists. And he continues to be a source of inspiration to students of human society in every part of the world.

[9] G. Charbonnier (ed.), *Conversations with Lévi-Strauss*, Jonathan Cape, 1969.

Durkheim not only preached comparative sociology, as so many before and after him have done, but practised it with great distinction. He believed that the same methods should be used for studying all types of societies, and himself applied them to the study of totemism among the Australian aborigines, rates of suicide among contemporary Europeans and forms of solidarity in ancient and modern civilizations. No other student of Western societies had Durkheim's insight into primitive societies, and in this he had few rivals even among the anthropologists of his time.

The true significance of Durkheim's work lies in the fact that it was a product of collective endeavour. Durkheim had collected around himself a band of scholars who shared a certain conception of human society and a certain method of sociological inquiry. They worked in close association with each other and investigated societies of diverse kinds. The results of these investigations were published in the journal *L'Année Sociologique* which stands as a remarkable testimony to the unity of sociology and social anthropology.

The *Année Sociologique* was established in 1898 and discontinued in 1913. It was during this period that the French school of sociology acquired its distinctive shape. Durkheim and his associates were not fieldworkers in the modern sense, and this in a way made it easier for them to discuss a wider range of societies than is generally done today by those who collect their own empirical material: I have mentioned earlier the part played by empirical investigations in bringing about a separation between sociology and social anthropology in Britain and the United States.

Whereas students of human society in the Anglo-Saxon countries were at that time interested mainly in the study of two types of society, the tribal or very primitive and the industrial or very advanced, members of the *Année Sociologique* group were, in addition, interested in the ancient civilizations—Bouglé was a Sanskritist, Granet a Sinologist—and to that extent their outlook was more truly comparative. Their studies make it clear to us today that if the science of society is to be divided according to the types of society being studied, then logically we will need not two but three or more subdivisions.

After Durkheim's death the study of society and culture took a new turn in France. The distinction between sociology and ethnology reasserted itself. In the inter-War years Marxism became a major influence in French sociology and this influence continues to the present time. Durkheim's nephew and collaborator, Marcel Mauss, sought to continue the tradition of the *Année Sociologique*, but his influence remained strong only among ethnologists (or students of primitive and ancient societies) and declined among sociologists (or students of contemporary Western societies).

Today probably the two most influential students of society and culture in France are Raymond Aron and Claude Lévi-Strauss. Their work strikingly exemplifies the separation between sociology and anthropology, the very separation the *Année Sociologique* sought to overcome. Aron is an ardent advocate of comparative sociology, but for him this means in practice the comparison of the variants of industrial society. Lévi-Strauss is also a practitioner of the comparative method, but uses it only for the comparison of primitive societies and cultures. And although Aron began his trilogy[10] on industrial society by holding up *Les Structures élémentaires de la Parenté* as a model of sociological inquiry,[11] he did not make any further reference to the ideas of Lévi-Strauss in the rest of this work.

I have argued that it is one thing to advocate the merits of the comparative method, and another to practise this method in the full sense of the term. In Europe and America there has been a strong tendency to dichotomize the world into the primitive and the civilized, and this tendency has been a more potent factor in determining the actual division of work among students of society and culture than any ideal design for a 'comparative sociology'.

How then should we view the relationship between sociology and social anthropology in contemporary India? We have emphasized at several points the distinction between the ideal designs people construct —whether for the study of primitive or advanced societies, or for a comparative sociology—and the way they actually do their work. A realistic discussion of these two subjects—or these two branches of the same subject—must keep in mind the actual work that sociologists and social anthropologists in India have been doing and are likely to do.

The first point to note is that both sociology and social anthropology as we know them now were brought to India from outside, particularly from Britain. British scholars who lived in India or came

[10] Raymond Aron, *Dix-huit Leçons sur la Société industrielle*, Gallimard, 1962; *La Lutte de Classes*, Gallimard, 1964; *Democratie et Totalitarisme*, Gallimard, 1965.

[11] Aron, 1962, op. cit., p. 24.

as visitors helped these subjects to get off the ground. Later, Indian scholars trained abroad—mainly in Britain and the U.S.A.—played a leading part in developing studies of society and culture in India. While these scholars added a great deal to our understanding of Indian society and culture, their general theoretical orientations were, with few exceptions, largely those of scholars in Britain and America.

As branches of academic learning, sociology and anthropology were divided almost from the very beginning in their formal set-up in India. They began to be taught as separate subjects in Indian universities a little over fifty years ago. Bombay University started with sociology and Calcutta University with anthropology. For more than two decades these remained the primary centres of teaching and research in the subjects. Later, as new departments came up, universities in the eastern region opted for anthropology and those in the western region generally for sociology. In several of the new universities there are now separate departments for the two subjects although Calcutta has only a Department of Anthropology and Bombay only a Department of Sociology.

Anthropology is usually taught in Faculties of Science whereas sociology is taught in Faculties of Arts (or of Social Sciences). This distinction is carried over into the organization of research institutions and associations. The Indian Science Congress has a section for archaeology and anthropology but none for sociology. There has been since British days an Anthropological Survey of India corresponding to similar organizations in the fields of archaeology, botany, zoology and geology; there never has been an organization of this kind for sociological research.

The division of work that was proposed between anthropology and sociology half a century ago—and is still manifest in much of the formal set-up—reflected in a fairly exact way the distinctions then prevalent in Britain between the two subjects. Anthropologists were to study tribal customs and sociologists were to study the advanced sections of Indian society. It was no accident that W. H. R. Rivers was chosen to be the first head of the Department of Anthropology at Calcutta,[12] and the Department of Sociology at Bombay was launched by the urban sociologist, Patrick Geddes. No two students of human society could be further removed in their actual work than Geddes and Rivers.

[12] Rivers did not actually join the Department but died shortly before it was formally established.

But whatever the nature of the formal set-up, the actual development of studies in human society and culture followed a different course in India from the ones followed in the West. We have seen how in France the division between ethnology and sociology reasserted itself in spite of the attempts made through the *Année Sociologique* to assert the unity of all studies of society and culture. In India, on the other hand, social anthropologists and sociologists have continually interchanged roles in spite of attempts to separate the two in the formal academic structure.

The vague and arbitrary nature of the line separating the two subjects becomes at once evident when we examine the work done by sociologists and social anthropologists in India. The scholars who have contributed most to the understanding of Indian society and culture are precisely those who have consistently ignored the compartmentalization of Indian society into primitive and advanced sections. This compartmentalization is the true source of the distinction between social anthropology and sociology; once it is set aside, the distinction becomes difficult to sustain.

It is an interesting fact that G. S. Ghurye, who has probably had the longest and most successful career as a Professor of Sociology at an Indian university, was himself trained by the anthropologist, W. H. R. Rivers. The range of Ghurye's interests as well as the continuity between them is best represented in his collection of essays entitled *Anthropo-Sociological Papers*.[13] These essays cover a vast field between dual organization and cross-cousin marriage at one end and the social and economic conditions of clerks in Bombay city at the other.

Ghurye has not only conducted and promoted studies of all sections of contemporary Indian society; he has sought also to examine the basic features of traditional Indian civilization. His book on caste, in its several incarnations,[14] combines interests which in Britain or America would normally be pursued separately by anthropologists, sociologists and historians. In this sense Ghurye's work fits well into the design of the *Année Sociologique*, with the difference that the French sociologists were studying societies in all parts of the world whereas Ghurye has confined his interests mainly—though by no means solely—to India.

[13] G. S. Ghurye, *Anthropo-Sociological Papers*, Popular Prakashan, 1963.
[14] Originally published as *Caste and Race in India*, Routledge and Kegan Paul, 1932.

We find the same combination of interests in the work of N. K. Bose, who occupied broadly the same position among anthropologists at Calcutta as Ghurye does among sociologists at Bombay. Bose had an abiding interest in the tribal people of India, an interest which took him first to the Department of Anthropology at Calcutta University and which he developed later as Director of the Anthropological Survey of India and as Commissioner for Scheduled Castes and Scheduled Tribes. But far from believing that the tribal people of India were so distinctive as to require a separate discipline for their study, he emphasized the essential similarity and continuity between the tribal and the non-tribal people of the subcontinent. And since he was a great believer in the unity of scientific method, he applied the same method to the study of all sections of Indian society, 'primitive' as well as 'advanced'.

Bose's analyses of contemporary Indian society were based on a substantial body of fieldwork. He believed that anthropology was a field science and placed primary emphasis on direct observation in the study of social and cultural life. His fieldwork was, however, rather different from that of contemporary British or American anthropologists. He preferred what may be called extensive as opposed to intensive fieldwork, and felt that this was better suited to the requirements of an Indian social scientist studying different sections of his own society. This enabled Bose to spread his fieldwork over a remarkably wide range: at one end a careful investigation of the Juang tribe of Orissa and at the other a detailed survey of Calcutta city.[15]

The framework of Bose's work is best represented in his book, *Hindu Samajer Garan.*[16] Here again a combination of the perspectives of ethnology, sociology and Indology is revealed. Bose maintained that in order to understand fully any segment of Indian society its relation to the whole design of this society must be seen. Hence the study of tribes in the hills involved the study of castes in the plains, just as the study of castes in the villages led to the study of classes in the cities.

The same unity of approach can be observed in the work of the next

---

[15] His Juang work is described in several of his Bengali and English writings, e.g. *Cultural Anthropology*, Asia, 1961, and *Culture and Society in India*, Asia, 1967; his Calcutta survey was published as *Calcutta 1964, A Social Survey*, Lalvani, 1968.

[16] Available only in its original Bengali version published by Vishwabharati Granthalaya, 1356 (Bengali calendar).

generation of Indian scholars, notably M. N. Srinivas, S. C. Dube and Ramkrishna Mukherjee. Srinivas, as a pupil first of Ghurye and then of Radcliffe-Brown, has consistently emphasized the unity of social anthropology and sociology.[17] Both Dube and Mukherjee were trained in Departments of Anthropology, but they have both addressed themselves to what would be regarded in the West as properly socio-logical problems. Dube has studied bureaucracy, communications and the problems of social change in general.[18] Mukherjee has applied sophisticated quantitative techniques to the study of various aspects of Indian society,[19] having earlier contributed to a study of social mobility in Britain.[20]

A historian of ideas writing a hundred years from now might find it strange that students of society and culture in India first set up a distinction between social anthropology and sociology, and then went about almost systematically violating the distinction. We have seen already that the distinction did not originate in this country but was brought to it from outside. We must now examine the specific reasons which make it unworkable in Indian conditions. Only then will we be able to ask whether the distinction itself is logical or not.

The distinction between sociology and social anthropology (or cul-tural anthropology, or ethnology) thrives on a dichotomous view of the world. Whites and natives, civilized and primitive, us and they: this, historically, has been the basis of the distinction made in the West between the two. But given the way in which Indian society is con-stituted, it provides very little basis for generating—or sustaining—this kind of dichotomous distinction.

In India, unlike in America or Australia, the distinction between tribal and non-tribal society is vague, unclear and, in the end, arbi-trary. If we go by the textbooks, it will be hard to find many groups that conform to the anthropologist's definition of tribe.[21] The larger Indian tribes like the Santals, Oraons, Bhils and Gonds are certainly

---

[17] His approach is best exemplified in his *Caste in Modern India and Other Essays*, Asia, 1962.

[18] See, for instance, his most recent book, *Explanation and Management of Change*, Tata McGraw-Hill, 1971.

[19] See, for instance, his *The Sociologist and Social Change in India*, Prentice-Hall of India Ltd., 1965.

[20] D. V. Glass (ed.), *Social Mobility in Britain*, Routledge and Kegan Paul, 1954.

[21] For a good example of this see Marshal D. Sahlins, *Tribesmen*, Prentice-Hall, 1968.

very different from the tribes studied by anthropologists in America and Australia. Undoubtedly they had their distinctive customs, but all communities in India, and not just tribes, had and in a sense were encouraged to have distinctive customs.

The larger tribes practise settled agriculture. Their technology is a little more backward and the land they cultivate a little less fertile than of the non-tribal people. Otherwise there is much basic similarity between the two categories of people in their modes of livelihood and economic organization. Clearly, one who has studied an Oraon village in Chota Nagpur does not need to change his discipline when he goes to study a caste-Hindu village in Birbhum district. Indeed it is very likely that he will in the normal course find some non-tribal people in the Chota Nagpur village and some tribal people in the Birbhum village.

The tribal people have been for centuries linked by social, economic and political ties with the non-tribal people of India. This is true of even the remote hill tribes, although in their case the links were generally fewer and not always direct. What N. K. Bose sought to establish should by now be clear to all—that the differences between Juangs, Mundas, Oraons, Oilpressers, Blacksmiths, Weavers and Cultivators are differences of degree and not of kind. We can, of course, for practical purposes, draw a line and separate Juangs, Mundas and Oraons from the others; but we must always remember that the line will be arbitrary and will have significance only for the purpose for which it is drawn.

But if we cannot draw a line near one end, can we not draw it near the other—a line which will separate our emerging urban-industrial society from all that is set in a traditional mould? For surely, the sociologist would wish to prove his mettle by studying not rural society —whether tribal or non-tribal—but the complexities of industrial life in the city. We must see if the Indian city does not provide an altogether different field of investigation, calling for a different approach, a different method, different techniques and different concepts—in short, a different discipline.

But again, we cannot but be struck by the continuities between urban and rural life in India—the urban family and the rural family, city politics and village politics, urban and rural patterns of stratification. After all, it would be surprising if it were otherwise, for city and village have co-existed in India for more than two millennia. And if industrialization generates new social arrangements—as it undoubtedly does—here too the difference is one of degree rather than of kind. This is why many of those who started by studying rural India, like N. K. Bose or D. N. Majumdar, found it natural at some stage to turn their attention to urban India. If we are to develop a more adequate methodology for urban sociology in India, we will have to build on these beginnings.

We saw earlier that in the West a certain division of work between students of primitive and advanced societies has crystallized into the academic distinction between social (or cultural) anthropology and sociology. In India, in spite of the formal acceptance of this distinction, the actual pattern of work tends to lay stress on the unity of society and of culture. Which of these two patterns of work is the more logical?

It must be said first of all that what we are dealing with is less a disagreement over principle than a difference in patterns of work. Even in regard to actual patterns of work the difference must not be over-stressed. The case of the American sociologist Lloyd Warner, who was a pupil of Radcliffe-Brown, is instructive if not characteristic. He first made a study of the Murngin, an Australian aboriginal tribe, and then applied the lessons learnt in the field to the study of Newburyport, a modern American town.

In more recent times Erving Goffman, who turned from anthropology to sociology, has been an outstanding practitioner of the comparative approach. One could easily multiply examples from both Britain and the United States. But what is really important is that the more closely one examines the matter, the more difficult it becomes to draw a clear line on any logical basis between the two types of investigation into human societies and cultures.

No doubt the argument will continue as to whether there should be one unified discipline of sociology or two separate, though related, disciplines of social anthropology and sociology. Those who argue for a single, unified discipline will agree that the study of various societies will require various techniques of investigation and analysis. And those who maintain that, despite our ultimate aims and objectives, two separate subjects in fact exist and must continue to exist, will in their turn agree that there are very close relations between the two.

My own view is that whether we regard social anthropology and sociology as the same subject, or as different branches of the same subject, or as two different subjects will ultimately depend on how we feel about the varieties of human society and culture. If we feel that the similarities between them are more fundamental than their differences, we will be more inclined to accept the unity of social anthropology and sociology. If, on the other hand, we feel that their differences are more basic than their similarities, we will be more ready to accept the division between the two subjects. I am prepared to concede that there is no more scientific justification for accepting the first than the second point of view; ultimately it is a question of values.

2

Peasant Studies and their Significance

THE STUDY OF peasant communities, or of peasantry in the broad sense, is of major interest to sociologists and social anthropologists today. In this sense their present field of interest is somewhat different from what it was a hundred years ago. Sociologists and social anthropologists started by studying complex industrial societies at one end and primitive tribal societies at the other. By moving into the field of peasant studies they are seeking to make their investigations into the nature and types of human society more comprehensive if not complete.

Students of human society discovered not only a new field of study, but one which called upon them to combine the traditional skills of social anthropology and of sociology. From the viewpoint of comparative sociology an interesting feature of peasants is that they have, on the one hand, an elaborate system of kinship and marriage, and are, on the other, part of a complex system of stratification and class.

As noted earlier, social anthropologists have from the very beginning paid special attention to the study of kinship systems. It is not as if they have not studied other institutional systems. But these studies they have from the very beginning shared to some extent with others, whereas kinship studies is the one area of investigation which they have made their very own. Sociology in the narrow sense paid little attention to the systematic study of the relations of kinship and marriage outside the limited sphere of the family system. The reason for this is not far to seek. The study of 'advanced' industrial societies does not call for detailed analysis of the relations of kinship and affinity, for in these societies the scope of such relations is greatly restricted. On the other hand, the study of 'primitive' tribal societies demands the analysis of the kinship system which often provides the basic design for these societies.

Now the kinship system, though not coterminous with the whole community, plays a very significant part in peasant social life. No analysis of it can be complete which does not go into the details of the differentiation of social roles according to the ties of blood and marriage. In India the student of peasant social organization, no matter what his area of special interest, must look into the structure of corporate groups like the lineage and the nature of interpersonal relations among agnates, cognates and affines. This is even more manifestly the case for pre-Communist China; the available studies of peasant communities in China do in fact give a prominent place to clan, lineage and kinship.

If the study of kinship and marriage gave to traditional anthropology its specific concerns, classical sociology acquired its distinctive character from the study of class and stratification. Once again, this is not to deny the other interests of sociologists but only to observe that what distinguished classical sociology from all other disciplines, and more particularly anthropology, was its preoccupation with the problems of inequality. It is not difficult to see why sociologists paid so much attention to class and stratification and why social anthropologists neglected them. Sociology became a discipline mainly through the study of Western industrial societies. These societies, which drew the interest of the vast majority of sociologists, were, unlike those studied by the anthropologists, characterized by the presence of groups and categories which were elaborately ranked and between which there were visible conflicts of interest. The sociologist could no more ignore class and stratification than the anthropologist could ignore kinship and marriage.

Peasant studies not only involve the analysis of kinship and marriage but also require an understanding of stratification and class. Firstly, peasants are internally subdivided in terms of income and size of holding into, let us say, poor, middle and rich peasants; in India they might, in addition, be divided into different castes. But what is more important is that they form only one stratum or class in a complex system of classes and strata; no understanding of the peasants can be complete unless we see them in relation to non-working landowners on the one hand and landless workers on the other.

The study of peasant communities by sociologists and social anthropologists is of fairly recent origin. The first full-length community studies began to be published just before the Second War, and it is only during the last two decades that they have acquired their present significance. Among social anthropologists in the West peasant studies are gradually coming to acquire the position enjoyed by tribal studies in the years before the War. Part of the interest of contemporary Western scholars in the peasantry is fed by the awareness of the growing importance of the Third World. India, China and the countries of Africa and Latin America were till the end of the War of interest mainly to historians and ethnographers, i.e. scholars who recorded unfamiliar customs from either the past or the present. But with the end of the colonial era these countries have assumed a much more immediate contemporary relevance in the world as a whole. Not unreasonably, many people in the West have begun to feel that the best way to understand them is to investigate the social, economic and political problems of their peasantry.

The study of peasant communities is also a part of the process of self-awareness in the Third World itself. Asian, African and Latin American countries are now no longer entirely dependent for sociological investigations on scholars from the advanced nations. They are now producing their own sociologists for whom the study of peasant communities is naturally becoming a major undertaking. This field has both a theoretical and a practical side. On the practical side it is intimately associated with programmes of development and modernization. The peasantry has been for centuries characterized as backward and conservative. Much of the economic backwardness and social conservatism of the countries of the Third World has for long been attributed to the innate characteristics of the peasantry. As these countries embark on programmes of development and modernization it becomes necessary to discover the most effective means of changing their conditions of life. In both China and India rural development programmes have played an important part in creating interest in the study of peasant communities.

In very recent times a somewhat different image of the peasantry has emerged in certain quarters. This is what one might describe as the revolutionary as opposed to the conservative image, where the true repository of revolutionary potential in the Third World is considered to be the peasantry; any major revolution here must be rooted in the social and political situation of the peasantry. For this reason

3

the conditions of life of the peasantry, and peasant movements and associations are becoming important subjects of investigation in Asia and Latin America. Needless to say, these subjects become the concern of both enthusiasts of revolutionary change and experts in 'revolutionary prophylaxis'.

The field of peasant studies is rather vaguely defined. This is partly because the field itself is relatively new, and partly because the approaches to it are many and varied. Students of economic processes and of social institutions have somewhat different—though not necessarily contradictory—perspectives on the problem. The concept of 'peasant economy' developed by Chayanov and his school is being revived by some contemporary students of the peasantry.[1] A somewhat different orientation is to be found among the generality of social anthropologists whose interest is in the study of 'peasant society and culture'.

Corresponding to these differences in orientation there are differences in the use of concepts. Even among sociologists and social anthropologists there is no general agreement about the meanings attached to such terms as 'peasantry', 'peasant community' and 'peasant society'.[2] Anthropologists are sometimes inclined to use 'peasant society' as a residual category, putting together all kinds of societies which are neither clearly 'tribal' nor clearly 'industrial'. This is a source of confusion because, while peasants might share certain common characteristics throughout the world, the so-called peasant societies differ very much from each other. These questions will have to be disucssed in Chapter 3. Perhaps it will be better for the time being to consider agrarian rather than peasant societies, and to discuss peasant communities wherever these are found within this broad category of societies.

Despite their many limitations and ambiguities, studies of peasant communities have come to stay in sociology and social anthropology. Indeed, in Asian countries it is to these studies that the science of society owes much of its present shape. By basing themselves on the study of the peasantry, students of social life in these countries can by-pass the distinction between sociology and social anthropology which has bedevilled Western scholars for generations.

[1] See, for instance, A. V. Chayanov, *The Theory of Peasant Economy*, edited by Daniel Thorner, B. Kerblay and R. E. F. Smith, Irwin, 1966.

[2] For a recent discussion see Teodor Shanin (ed.), *Peasants and Peasant Societies*, Penguin, 1971, particularly the Introduction.

A sufficiently large number of studies of peasant communities from all over the world are now available to make some kind of stock-taking a worthwhile exercise. We shall begin with a consideration of the circumstances under which peasant studies by sociologists and social anthropologists came into being. We shall then discuss some of the major findings of these studies, particularly from the Asian countries. A great deal can be learned by comparing the Indian with the Chinese studies made in the field. We shall conclude with a brief discussion of similar studies of European peasant communities.

Several intellectual streams have contributed to the present interest among social anthropologists in the study of peasant communities. From the viewpoint of the discipline, the work of Redfield and his associates occupies a unique position. Redfield not only gave a new direction to anthropology in the United States, but also influenced significantly the work of scholars in Latin America, India and to some extent also China. British anthropologists held out against the new wave for some time, but the study of peasant communities has come to occupy an increasingly important place in their work in recent times.

Redfield's book on Tepoztlan[3] was the first full-length study of a peasant community using modern anthropological techniques of research. In the thirties Redfield made further empirical studies of Mexican communities and set a new trend of research among his American colleagues. It did not take anthropologists long to realize that a vast new field was lying unexplored, and Redfield turned their attention to it at a particularly opportune moment, when the possibilities of tribal studies within the United States were becoming more and more exhausted.

The work of Redfield and his colleagues helped to create a new image of anthropology. Anthropology could no longer be described as 'the investigation of oddments by the eccentric'.[4] It is true that the work of Malinowski and his associates had paved the way for a more realistic and down-to-earth appraisal of tribal societies. But these societies were still too remote and far away to have much more than an exotic appeal to the intelligentsia in America, Europe or even Asia.

[3] Robert Redfield, *Tepoztlan, a Mexican Village: A Study of Folk Life*, University of Chicago Press, 1930.
[4] Clyde Kluckhohn, cited in Max Gluckman, *Politics, Law and Ritual in Tribal Societies*, Basil Blackwell, 1965.

The study of peasant communities brought anthropology to the doorstep of all students of society and culture in the Third World.

The study of peasant communities not only gave anthropology access to a substantial section of the world's population, but it also opened up a new approach to the understanding of civilizations. Field investigations and literary studies had become distinct and separate activities. The anthropologist studied tribal communities in the field; these communities were isolated, self-sufficient and devoid of any written records about their past. The historian and classicist studied civilizations by examining literary sources handed down from the past. Peasant communities required to be investigated in the field; but they were also parts of a larger civilization which had to be understood in order to make the investigation complete.

Redfield's own work in Mexico assembled a wealth of new empirical material. It revealed in simple, non-technical language the nature of peasant social structure and its links with the outside world. It also presented a vivid picture of the beliefs, values and attitudes of the Mexican peasant. The great merit of Redfield's empirical work was that it brought together material from tribal, peasant and urban communities.[5] By doing this he was able to link the study of peasant communities with the traditional concerns of social anthropology and sociology.

Redfield presented his empirical material in an attractive theoretical framework. The conception of a 'folk-urban continuum' enabled him to see Mexican society as a whole by examining it closely at certain crucial points. The remote tribal community, the peasant village, the small town and the larger urban centre bore a family resemblance to each other; but they represented different degrees of structural and cultural complexity.[6] The anthropologist was being offered at one and the same time a method for the study of peasant communities and a typology of various communities. In constructing this typology Redfield drew heavily on the work of nineteenth century sociologists such as Tönnies, Durkheim and Maine.

Redfield devoted his later writings to discussions of the little community in general and the peasant community in particular. His characterization of the social, cultural and psychological attributes of the peasantry has become justly famous. In the last book he wrote,

[5] In particular *The Folk Culture of Yucatan*, University of Chicago Press, 1941.

[6] Ibid.

Peasant Society and Culture,[7] he surveyed the empirical material on the peasantry brought together by anthropologists during the two preceding decades and on this basis tried to formulate the common characteristics of peasants throughout the world. Following Kroeber, Redfield defined peasants as being part-societies and part-cultures.[8] This is the characteristic anthropological definition which, viewing peasants in opposition to tribals, emphasizes their articulation with the wider society and culture. Economists, on the other hand, tend to view peasants in opposition to farmers, emphasizing their isolation from the wider market economy. Needless to say, there are several contemporary anthropologists who give a prominent place to isolation from the market in characterizing the peasantry.[9]

The work of Redfield and his associates underlined the organic character of the peasant community. Peasant social life is seen as being governed by certain common social values emphasizing the virtues of work, the obligations to kin and neighbours, and reverence for the supernatural. The peasant community is small and homogeneous, and the relations between its members have a direct and personal quality. The even tenor of peasant social life is not normally disturbed by the kinds of conflict and violence which are common features of urban industrial life. There is evidently a family resemblance between Redfield's picture of the peasant community and Tönnies's model of Gemeinschaft.

Other observers of peasant communities have found these conceptions idealized and perhaps slightly romantic. Closer analyses show such communities to be often sharply divided by conflicting interests.[10] Perhaps the limitation lay not so much in Redfield's empirical investigations as in his conceptual framework. When one seeks to understand peasant communities primarily in terms of a set of common values there is a tendency to represent them as harmonious. A more realistic representation must pay adequate attention to the material basis of peasant social life.[11]

[7] Robert Redfield, *Peasant Society and Culture, An Anthropological Approach to Civilization*, University of Chicago Press, 1956.   [8] Ibid.

[9] See, for instance, Eric Wolf, *Peasants*, Prentice-Hall, 1966.

[10] See, for instance, the restudy of Tepoztlan by Oscar Lewis in which a contrasting picture of the same village is presented. Oscar Lewis, *Life in a Mexican Village: Tepoztlan Restudied*, University of Illinois Press, 1951.

[11] André Béteille, 'Ideas and Interests: Some Conceptual Problems in the Study of Social Stratification in Rural India', *International Social Science Journal*, Vol. XXI, No. 2, 1969, pp. 219–34.

The field that was opened up by Redfield with his Mexican studies was soon extended into the Old World. After all, it is the principal Asian countries that have the largest number of peasant communities and have had them for the longest time. The Latin American peasantry by contrast is of relatively recent origin, and it has emerged under somewhat special conditions. In India and China peasant communities have existed in their natural condition for millennia. It is here that the study of peasant communities holds the promise of a living understanding of the world's most ancient civilizations.

There were other reasons behind the rapid growth of Western interest in the peasant communities of Asia. American social scientists have always been characterized by a practical approach to problems. They must have realized very quickly that in the post-colonial era Asia would become a major field of foreign policy interest in their own country. Consequently, the study of peasant society and culture in these countries was likely to receive vast governmental patronage. This of course is not to say that American social scientists working in the Third World have always allowed themselves to be used as instruments of American foreign policy.

Redfield himself was closely though indirectly associated with the study of peasantry in both China and India. Fei Hsiao-Tung was invited to the University of Chicago where, with the assistance of Mrs Redfield, he prepared his book on the Chinese gentry,[12] which was in a way complementary to his earlier work on peasant life in China. Redfield's influence on community studies in India made by both American and Indian scholars is well known; it was largely under his influence (and that of Milton Singer) that the studies brought together in *Village India* came into being.

But there were other sources of inspiration for peasant studies in Asia. It would be fair to say that the inter-War period was the time when Asian scholars began to take an active interest in their own peasantry, and some of them found the new anthropology a useful instrument which they sought to adapt to their own purpose. This was certainly the context in which anthropology was introduced into China, and this context has to be kept in mind if we are to understand the shape taken by the subject in India.

Countries like India and China have had an indigenous intelligentsia for centuries. Towards the end of the colonial era this intelligentsia, which was highly urbanized, found itself in a general way cut off from

[12] Fei Hsiago-Tung, *China's Gentry*, University of Chicago Press, 1953.

its own social and cultural roots. This was the time when a growing awareness emerged that the real Asia was the Asia of the villages. In India this awareness was most clearly articulated by Tagore and Gandhi, both of whom influenced the work of the anthropologist N. K. Bose. Bose sought to use his anthropological training to investigate problems which were brought to the surface by the nationalist movement;[13] outside anthropology there were of course other social scientists who were engaged in a similar venture.

As for China, Fei Hsiao-Tung describes how scholars like himself reacted against the inadequacies of traditional scholarship,[14] which was essentially literary and placed a kind of final value on the wisdom contained in the books. It served its purpose so long as the world was relatively unchanging and people more or less accepted the existing order of things. But in China, as in India, the vast social and economic changes of the twentieth century turned the attention of the scholars to peasants in the villages, and it was here that they found the traditional methods of scholarship inadequate. To understand peasant social life by living among the peasants through direct and systematic observation was something new which Western social science contributed to China.

The aims of Fei and his colleagues were largely those of social reconstruction. Their complaint against the traditional scholarship was that it provided very little guidance for practical action in a changing environment. They saw the problem of China as being rooted in the poverty, unemployment and exploitation of the peasantry. They were concerned about the disintegration of the traditional social order which had given the peasants some measure of security and well-being. They felt that the urgent task of social reconstruction called for the application of scientific methods to the understanding of social and economic processes. It was in this context that sociology and social anthropology began to take roots in pre-Communist China.

In India the relationship between social reconstruction and sociological investigation has been more complex. While centres such as Tagore's Sriniketan tried from the beginning to combine the two, the university departments in general took a more academic view of the problem. Further, social scientists in India were perhaps concerned

[13] N. K. Bose, *Culture and Society in India*, Asia, 1967.
[14] Fei Hsiao-Tung and Chang Chih-I, *Earthbound China, A Study of Rural Economy in Yunnan*, Routledge and Kegan Paul, 1949.

to a greater extent than their Chinese colleagues with the demands of their discipline so that we see in their work a more active and continuous preoccupation with concepts, methods and theories considered independently of social action.

The studies made in the thirties and forties by Chinese sociologists of peasant communities in China deserve attention for a variety of reasons. In spite of the very different paths taken by India and China since 1947, the two countries have a common background and a common set of social, economic and political problems which become particularly clear when we consider the situation of the peasantry. The similarities between the Chinese and the Indian peasantry are no less striking than their differences. Indian sociologists tend to ignore the fact that several village studies were made by Chinese sociologists and published during the decade before the Communist régime was established. A comparison of Chinese and Indian village studies will also provide an interesting exercise in the sociology of knowledge. The impact of Western ideas, including Western social science, was very different in the two countries. Chinese scholars took to village studies after a very brief exposure to Western sociology, whereas in India these studies came to be made after a relatively long acquaintance with British and American sociology and social anthropology. What differences do we find in the concepts, methods and theories applied to village studies in the two countries?

The first full-length study of a Chinese village was published in 1939 by Fei Hsiao-Tung.[15] This work was completed under the supervision of Malinowski at the London School of Economics and it carries a Foreword by him. In a later work[16] Fei has acknowledged his intellectual debt to two other scholars, Robert Park, the American sociologist and S. M. Shirokogoroff, the Russian ethnologist. These intellectual influences were used with discrimination and in the work itself there is no attempt to enter into the controversies then prevalent in Western sociology.

Fei's description of his village is presented in a matter-of-fact way without any effort to enter into conceptual or theoretical niceties. The principal objective was to observe carefully and record faithfully the different aspects of the social life of the community. One notices two

[15] Fei Hsiao-Tung, *Peasant Life in China*, Routledge and Kegan Paul, 1939.
[16] Fei Hsiao-Tung, 'Introduction' in Fei and Chang, *Earthbound China*, op. cit.

features of the framework of analysis which Malinowski had successfully established among his associates. The first was to show the social
and cultural activities of the peasants in their manifold interrelatedness. The second was to concentrate on the day-to-day life of the
people rather than on the colourful and the spectacular. Kiangts'un,
the village studied by Fei, is described in terms of the cycle of work or
economic activities, domestic life and the kinship system, and ceremonial life or the cycle of rituals. There is a close interdependence
between the three in Kiangts'un as in most peasant communities. The
unit of economic activities on the peasant farm is the peasant household, and most of the important ceremonies are connected with either
the cycle of economic activities or the domestic cycle of birth, marriage
and death.

A second full-length study of a different part of China was published
shortly afterwards: the account by Martin Yang of Taitou, the village in which he himself grew up in Shantung province.[17] Unlike
Kiangts'un, which was a rice-growing village, Taitou was located in
the wheat-growing region, and consequently there were differences
between the two in their patterns of agriculture. However, both villages were characterized by small holdings, and were in this way
basically similar in their productive systems, although the inhabitants
of Taitou depended solely on agriculture whereas those of Kiangts'un
combined agriculture with village industry.

Taitou was a village of small peasants. Yang divided its population
into four categories according to the amount of land held, and the
wealthiest families owned under ten acres each. Almost all adults,
both men and women, worked in the fields, although those who were
wealthy tended to withdraw from the heavier work as they advanced
in years. The village did not have a very elaborate division of labour.
There were only a few families of artisans. Blacksmiths, carpenters,
weavers, oil-pressers and masons did not constitute specialized groups
but were drawn from among the peasants themselves. Yang discusses
the peasant community in terms of the structure of its basic groups
and categories. He views social groups as being of different kinds, and
takes the family which is the 'most primary group' as his point of
departure. The village, unlike the family, is in his view a secondary
group. He shows how the family is structurally linked to the village
through various 'transitional groups' such as clans, neighbourhoods

[17] Martin Yang, *A Chinese Village: Taitou, Shantung Province*, Routledge and
Kegan Paul, 1948.

and other socio-economic and socio-religious groups. Finally he shows how the village is linked with the market town and with other villages served by the same market town.

In some ways the most characteristic among the studies of Chinese peasant communities is the set of three studies made by Fei Hsiao-Tung and Chang Chih-I and brought together in *Earthbound China*.[18] These three villages were selected, along with the one described in *Peasant Life in China*, to represent different types of productive arrangements, and their comparative study gives valuable insights into the broader economic forces at work in the Chinese countryside. It is unfortunate that the larger project of which these studies were a part, and whose design is briefly explained in Fei's Introduction to *Earthbound China*, had to remain incomplete.

Earthbound China is an attempt to explore systematically the institutional background of the Chinese rural economy. Fei relates the study of the three village communities to the earlier work of Tawney and of Buck. Certain important questions are raised on methodology, and, in particular, on how far it is possible to understand the social and economic organization of the Chinese farm through the methods of survey research. Fei has no difficulty in showing that Buck, who based his own important work on survey research, was misled on a number of fundamental points. In particular, he criticizes Buck for trying to understand the Chinese rural economy in terms of the 'conventional American classification into owners, part-owners and tenants'.[19] Tenancy in China meant something quite different from tenancy in America; and in China itself tenants of clan land and of individual land had very different obligations. An understanding of these important factors required intensive investigation by the methods of participant-observation. Students of the Indian village community will find familiar questions being raised here on the relative advantages of different methods of investigation.

In regard to typology, Fei urges caution over the use of generalized and abstract cultural categories. He maintains, quite reasonably, that the typology must reflect the basic interests of the investigation. The basic interests in this study are in poverty, landlessness, inefficient technology and the exploitation of the country by the town. The typology presented here is by no means exhaustive, for all the three

[18] Fei and Chang, *Earthbound China*, op. cit. Interestingly, Fei tells us that the title of the book was suggested by Malinowski before it was actually written.

[19] Ibid., p. 2.

villages are located in the same ecological region, far away from the centres of Chinese civilization. The book nevertheless provides a valuable introduction to an understanding of the economic and social problems of rural China.

All three Yunnan villages were characterized by small or dwarf holdings rarely exceeding ten acres. In all three most adult members of both sexes participated in some form of agricultural work. The division of labour between agriculture and handicraft was not very rigidly maintained. Individuals often combined a variety of occupational roles, either at the same time or at different stages in their life. There were also differences between the three communities. In the first village, Luts'un, most of the landowners were resident and their holdings were uniformly small. In the second village, Yits'un, there were several relatively large landowners possessing land in other villages, while others were small occupying owners; however, the land owned outside the village was often poor in quality and the returns from it were uncertain. The third community, Yuts'un, had many tenants while its big landowners lived outside in nearby towns. These three villages are compared with Kiangts'un, a community of tenants whose absentee landlords lived in large towns, this being described as 'a further development of tenancy than in the third type'.[20] The economic problems in the three Yunnan villages are discussed in the context of their social framework. The main emphasis in the discussion is naturally on the organization of work and the part played in it by the different categories of villagers. The family emerges once again as the primary unit of both production and consumption. The study concludes with a discussion of the best way of combining agriculture with rural industry so as to ensure viability for the farm family.

The work begun by Fei and his colleagues at the National Yunnan University had to be discontinued before the Communists came to power. There is little authentic sociological data on Chinese peasant communities after 1949. C. K. Yang's study of Nanching, a village on the fringe of Canton city, gives some idea of a peasant community during the transition from the old to the new social order.[21] This study once again emphasizes the distribution of land and the organization of production, and discusses the changes brought about in both during

[20] Ibid., p. 17.
[21] C. K. Yang, *A Chinese Village in Early Communist Transition*, Harvard University Press, 1959.

the first phase of land reforms. Thus, the village studies from China were not only all conducted within a brief period of time, but are all characterized by a certain unity of approach and a concern for certain common problems, those centring around the ownership, control and use of land.

Whereas in China village studies by sociologists virtually came to an end around 1949, in India it was only after Independence in 1947 that they were begun in a really serious way. Although India has had a longer and more continuous tradition of social science research, the first full-length sociological study of an Indian village was published as late as 1955, a decade and a half after the publication of Fei's book on Kiangts'un. Indian sociologists turned to the study of peasant communities after the discipline had become established in the country; for this reason we find a somewhat greater theoretical sophistication in their work than in the Chinese village studies.

Although Chinese and Indian village communities share many features in common, the emphases in the two sets of studies are somewhat different. The Chinese studies, as we have noted, focus the attention on the peasant and his farm, and on the social and economic consequences of fragmented holdings, tenancy and landlessness. These problems have until recently played a less important part in the studies made by sociologists and social anthropologists of Indian village communities. Part of this is no doubt due to the fact that in India a division of labour between economists and sociologists had already become established when village studies were begun by the latter.

We have, of course, a much more comprehensive picture of village communities in India than we have for China. We not only have studies covering almost all the major regions of India but these studies deal with almost every aspect of institutional life. An important reason for the variety of these studies is that they have been made by sociologists and social anthropologists not only from India but from all over the world.

The first full-length sociological study of an Indian village, by S. C. Dube, was published in 1955.[22] He had been trained as an anthropologist and earlier made a study of a small tribal group with a simple technology.[23] Dube's study of the village Shamirpet gave a clear indication of the new direction of research in Indian sociology. He empha-

[22] S. C. Dube, *Indian Village*, Routledge and Kegan Paul, 1955.
[23] S. C. Dube, *The Kamar*, Universal Publishers, 1951.

sized the need, first, to understand the internal heterogeneity of the non-tribal village, and, second, to examine it in its manifold relationship with the outside world.

We should remember that the first full-length study of an Indian village was the outcome of a very practical programme, viz. the Osmania University Social Service Extension Project. The study also benefited from and was to a certain extent shaped by the fact that the project was interdisciplinary in character. There were economists, agronomists and experts on health and nutrition in the team, whose work was done under the general supervision of Dube. Dube pursued his interest in the study of extension programmes by publishing a few years later a book on the social and cultural implications of the Community Development Programme.[24]

Dube's book on Shamirpet is in the style of the old anthropological monographs. It does not seek to focus attention on any particular problem or institutional system, but provides a general and comprehensive account of all the major areas of village life. There is first an account of the major social categories in the village in terms of religion and caste. Then there are descriptions of the economic system, the ritual system and the family system. The book concludes with a discussion of the changes coming about in the Indian village. We clearly get the impression that Dube's village is more complex and more highly stratified than the peasant communities studied by Fei.

An important landmark in the development of village studies in India was the publication in 1955 of a collection of eight essays edited by Marriott,[25] which provides descriptive accounts of villages in different parts of India. But more important than that, it raises fundamental questions of methodology. To what extent can the Indian village be treated as a social and cultural isolate? Given the fact that it is not wholly isolated, what kind of strategy should the anthropologist adopt in order to provide a meaningful account of it? The book was clearly designed to answer questions whose roots lay in the intellectual discipline of anthropology.

The studies brought together in *Village India* not only raised important questions of methodology but also generated a number of valuable concepts. In his essay on Rampura Srinivas put forward the important concept of the dominant caste which was to figure prominently in later writings on the Indian village. Marriott in his essay on

[24] S. C. Dube, *India's Changing Villages*, Routledge and Kegan Paul, 1958.
[25] McKim Marriott (ed.), *Village India*, University of Chicago Press, 1955.

Kishan Garhi formulated the two related concepts of 'universaliza-tion' and 'parochialization' with a view to interpreting the active relationship between the great and the little traditions.

The relatively high level of sophistication of the anthropologists who were studying rural India generated some technical and abstruse controversies such as that concerning the sociological reality of the Indian village. In a provocative article Dumont and Pocock wrote that the real problems of sociological analysis in India should centre around kinship, caste and religion, and that the Indian village lacked sociological reality;[26] Bailey wrote an effective rejoinder, defending the validity of taking the village as the basic unit of investigation.[27] Their relative lack of sophistication had protected the Chinese anthro-pologists from debates of this kind.

The eight essays brought together in *Village India* reveal clearly the structural diversity of village communities in the country. There are villages like Rampura in Mysore state which can be properly de-scribed as peasant communities. Here most of the land is owned by the Okkaligas who are a cultivating caste and constitute about half the population of the village. Most of the land is in small and medium holdings, and much of the production is organized on the basis of family labour with some use of hired labour for particular operations and on particular occasions. In contrast to Rampura is the village of Kumbapettai, described by Kathleen Gough, where the Brahmins constitute the dominant caste. Villages of the type of Kumbapettai— by no means rare in Tanjore or in India as a whole—have not only a more elaborate caste hierarchy but also a more complex structure of agrarian relations. Where Brahmins own most of the land, production is organized not on the basis of family labour but on the basis of either tenancy or wage labour. It is doubtful if villages like Kumba-pettai can be properly described as peasant communities, for the Brahmins who constitute the dominant group in such villages can hardly be characterized as peasants.

Village India (and its companion volume, *India's Villages*, published in the same year)[28] was followed by a succession of monographs on individual villages from different parts of the country. These mono-

[26] Louis Dumont and David F. Pocock, 'Village Studies', *Contributions to Indian Sociology*, No. 1, 1957.

[27] F. G. Bailey, 'For a Sociology of India?' *Contributions to Indian Sociology*, No. 3, 1959, pp. 88–101.

[28] M. N. Srinivas (ed.), *India's Villages*, Asia, 1960.

graphs tended to focus attention on particular aspects of village social structure. Thus some emphasized economic processes, others dwelt on kinship and yet others concentrated on ritual. But all of them gave a special place to the caste structure of the village as providing the basic framework of analysis.[29] In fact, the study of village social structure and of caste at the village level became almost synonymous, the village providing a convenient physical locus for the study of intercaste relations on the ground.

This overemphasis on caste among students of the Indian village led them to neglect one of the most crucial features of a peasant social and economic system, the technical and social organization of production. Because of the overwhelming influence of Redfield many of them characterized their work, rather vaguely, as the study of peasant communities. Yet if they had examined a little more closely the productive systems of the villages they were studying, they would have seen that these were not all communities of peasants, but were often divided into landlords, tenants and landless labourers.

An attempt had in fact been made nearly thirty years ago by Ramkrishna Mukherjee to study villages in the Indian subcontinent in terms of their productive organization.[30] And Mukherjee had begun by raising the question as to whether these could be regarded as communities of peasants. His aim was to marshal statistical evidence which would challenge the widely-prevalent myth of the egalitarian Indian village. Mukherjee's work was done before the partition of India, in the Bogra district of what is now Bangladesh. There was a long gap between his fieldwork and the publication of his material in book form. The published material itself has been presented in terms of highly formal categories, and we do not get from it the same insight into the working of village social life that we get from the Chinese monographs or from the later Indian monographs. For these and other reasons Mukherjee's studies did not make a substantial impact on the work taken up by the next generation of sociologists and social anthropologists in rural India.

It is now almost twenty years since the first studies of the Indian village using caste as the basic frame of reference began to be published. During this period almost every aspect of caste as it operates at the village level has been explored. There are signs that the new

[29] Béteille, 'Ideas and Interests', op. cit.

[30] Ramkrishna Mukherjee, *Six Villages of Bengal*, Popular Prakashan, 1971; also *The Dynamics of a Rural Society*, Akademie Verlag, 1957.

generation of sociologists would like to turn from caste to the study of the relations centring around the ownership, control and use of land. It might be worth their while at this juncture to look at the work which had been done with so much patience and care—and under such difficult conditions—by their predecessors in China.

Peasant communities are found not only in Asia, Africa and Latin America, but also in most of the European countries. The peasantry did not attract much attention from the founders of European sociology with a few exceptions; they were believed to be a declining force in the face of the newly-emerging industrial social order. However, in several East European countries the peasants constitute a substantial section of the population even today. In countries like Italy, France and Austria also, the peasant question is an important one both economically and politically.[31]

The 'peasant question' has of course held the attention of European scholars for several generations, but in Western Europe in particular it has been a question more in the realm of economic history than of sociology or anthropology. The issues in the study of the European peasantry were either economic, centring around inadequate technology, low productivity and declining consumption; or political, centring around peasant conservatism and the role of the peasant lobby in national politics. The techniques developed by Redfield for understanding a civilization through the study of peasant communities were rarely applied in the European countries. Hence we know much about the economic and political problems of the European peasantry but less about their social and cultural characteristics.

We now have a few full-length studies by social anthropologists of European peasant communities. One of the first was a study made by an American anthropologist, Joel Halpern, of a Serbian village in Yugoslavia.[32] Orasac, the village described by Halpern, is a typical peasant community in which the family farm is the centre of social and economic life. Unlike the case in many Indian villages, land is fairly equitably distributed so that there are no large landowners and few landless agricultural labourers. Those who own land cultivate it generally by their own labour and the labour of their family members; those who own no land generally work for wages outside agriculture.

[31] For a useful recent discussion see S. H. Franklin, *The European Peasantry, The Final Phase*, Methuen, 1969.

[32] Joel M. Halpern, *A Serbian Village*, Columbia University Press, 1958.

This picture of a relatively homogeneous community of people with small family holdings on which both men and women work is confirmed by other available studies of peasant villages in both East and West Europe.[33] A recent study of a Hungarian village, Atany, by two Hungarian anthropologists, examines in detail work, leisure and family life among what the authors describe as 'proper peasants'.[34] Here also the family farm, on which both men and women do the work, constitutes the basic unit of social and economic life in the village.

It is not as if Orasac and Atany, any more than other peasant villages whether in East or West Europe, are fully egalitarian communities. There are rich and poor, landowning and landless people among them. But these are differences of degree rather than of kind. For all those who live on the land do much the same kind of work, and there is no unbridgeable gulf separating the rich landowners from the landless poor. It is only where the landowners become a permanent, self-perpetuating, non-working stratum and the landless are virtually cut off from all means of ownership or control of the land that we approach the negation of a peasant community.

[33] For West Europe see F. G. Bailey (ed.), *Gifts and Poison: The Politics of Reputation*, Basil Blackwell, 1971.
[34] Edit Fel and Tamas Hofer, *Proper Peasants: Traditional Life in a Hungarian Village*, Aldine Publishing Co., 1969.

3

The Concept of Peasant Society

THE DISCOVERY of the peasantry as a vast new field of investigation gave a dramatic turn to the development of sociology and social anthropology towards the middle of the present century. Social anthropology in particular acquired a new lease of life in the United States and Britain through studies of peasant communities in different parts of the world. If the primitive tribes had disappeared or were in the process of disappearing, there was a virtually inexhaustible supply of peasant communities in Asia, Latin America, Africa and even Europe.

It must be remembered that the anthropological understanding of the peasantry was achieved mainly through community studies. It was natural for students of these peasant communities to feel, as pioneers, that they were discovering—or at least exploring—a new kind of society of which the communities they studied were the building-blocks. Perhaps it was also natural on their part to claim that peasant societies predominated in almost every major region in the world. In this way countries as different as India and Ethiopia or Brazil and Yugoslavia came to be included in that vast and amorphous sociological category, the peasant society.

Now I am going to argue that it is one thing to talk about peasant communities in India (or China) and another to characterize Indian (or Chinese) society as a whole as a peasant society. There are peasant communities in both India and Yugoslavia, and a comparison of these will tell us something about the nature and types of communities. But it would be misleading to use this comparison as a basis for making statements about similarities and differences between Indian and Yugoslav societies.

The so-called peasant societies are sometimes very complex and highly stratified. They frequently include groups, classes and categories which cannot in any acceptable sense be regarded as peasants. Even where peasants are numerically preponderant the non-peasant strata may play a significant, or even decisive, part in the society taken as a whole. Further, the nature and role of these non-peasant strata may differ greatly from one society to another. Consequently, what are called peasant societies might share very little in common apart from the organizational features of one particular type of community.

Leaving aside altogether the contrast between urban and rural communities, it should be clear that in countries like India not all rural communities are communities of peasants. Indian villages, as we have seen, differ greatly in their structural type. There are some like Kumbapettai in which an elaborate hierarchy of caste is matched by an elaborate agrarian hierarchy. There are others like Rampura whose inhabitants are mainly smallholders belonging to the middle-level castes and who themselves cultivate the land. By applying the blanket term 'peasant community' to all of these we obscure significant differences in the types of agrarian structure in rural India.

The idea that village India is the physical locus of a peasant society seems to be the tacit assumption of a large number of sociologists and social anthropologists working in the Indian field. It is difficult to say how far Redfield himself would subscribe to this idea, but it is very much in evidence in the work of his followers both in India and abroad. While it may be useful to characterize some societies as peasant societies, it is doubtful whether one could properly do this in the case of traditional India with its elaborate caste hierarchy on the one hand and its complex agrarian stratification on the other.

The conceptual scheme which I would like to submit to critical examination can be seen in the form in which academic seminars on Indian society are often organized. It is common for such seminars to be divided into three sections, dealing with Urban Society, Peasant Society and Tribal Society. One can see at once the logic behind the scheme. Indian society is divided first into an urban and a rural sector. The rural sector is then divided into a tribal and a non-tribal sector. The non-tribal villages make up the peasant sector of Indian society.

Unfortunately, this rather facile scheme tends to be followed in the teaching of social anthropology in various universities. Students are taught something about urban India and tribal India, and then the rest of rural India is treated as if it constituted a society of peasants. This leaves them without any clear idea about the elaborate agrarian hierarchy which prevailed in traditional India and persists in many parts of the country even now. Further, some of the village studies through which 'peasant society' in India is illustrated are not studies of peasants alone, but of very heterogeneous communities.

One can see the shadow of Redfield's conceptual scheme in the division of Indian society into urban, peasant and tribal, but there is something basically unsatisfactory in the scheme as applied to India. Firstly, 'peasant society' as conceived in it is a residual category, and it has all the disadvantages of any residual category. It is conceived not in terms of any positive attributes, but as that sector of rural India which remains after the exclusion of tribal society. Part of this is due to the way in which sociology and social anthropology have developed in the West. We have seen that initially the former was concerned with industrial or urban and the latter with primitive or tribal societies. The middle ground, which had hitherto remained uncovered, was willy-nilly given the name of peasant society.

Secondly, while the non-tribal village is often too highly stratified to merit the name of peasant community, many of the so-called tribal villages in India are in fact communities of peasants. If we leave aside the small, nomadic, hunting and gathering tribes, we will find that many of the larger tribes that live by settled agriculture are organized into communities which correspond very well to the classic conception of peasantry. I would go even further and argue that if one is looking for peasant communities in India the best place to begin would be among the Santals, the Oraons and the Mundas. In fact what I am suggesting is that we not only take a more critical look at our concept of peasant society but that we also thoroughly re-examine the tribe-peasant distinction around which much of our anthropological discussion seems to centre.

It should be emphasized that the issues involved are not merely terminological but substantive. It is not as if a particular sector of Indian society has been wrongly labelled as 'peasant society', and by giving it a different and more appropriate label our problem will be solved. I am also far from suggesting that the label 'peasant society' should now be attached to what we have been describing as 'tribal society' while a new label is thought out for the remainder of rural society.

My purpose is not to obscure the very real differences that exist among rural communities in India but to throw light on their true nature. The roots of these differences lie in a variety of factors among which the most important appear to be the distribution of land, the tenurial system, the structure of caste and the organization of work, including its division between men and women. An analysis of these will give a much deeper understanding of the varieties of rural communities in India than the use of blanket categories like 'peasant society' and 'tribal society'.

What should we mean by 'peasants' or 'peasantry'? *Chamber's Twentieth Century Dictionary* describes a peasant as 'a countryman: a rustic: one whose occupation is rural labour', and peasantry as 'the body of peasants or tillers of the soil: rustics: labourers'. In the English language—and also in other European languages—there appears to be an association between village life and a life of labour. In pre-industrial Europe gentlefolk lived not in villages but in manors, towns and cities. It would be dangerous to assume the validity of this kind of association for every society and culture. The *Shorter Oxford English Dictionary* defines a peasant as 'one who lives in the country and works on the land; a countryman, a rustic'. It adds in parentheses that in early use it referred properly only to people of foreign countries, 'often connoting the lowest rank, antithetical to *noble*'. It certainly had a derogatory connotation in Elizabethan English—'Oh what a rogue and peasant slave am I'—which it seems to retain in part even now. *Webster's Third New International Dictionary* describes the peasant as being of a class 'that tills the soil as small free landowners or hired labourers'. Webster points out that peasants are chiefly an European class, presumably with a view to underlining the contrast between Europe and North America. An additional meaning is given of the peasant as being 'a rather uneducated uncouth person in the low income group'.

In ordinary usage the term peasant has several closely related connotations among which I would now like to identify three. Firstly, the peasant is attached to the land. He not only lives on the land but by his labour makes the land bear fruit. The legal relation of the peasant to the land might vary. He might be an owner, a tenant or, in the limiting case, a labourer without any right of ownership or occupancy; but in all cases he earns his livelihood by labour. Within this framework one might give a broader or narrower connotation to the term. Some would limit it to owner-cultivators while others would include tenants and landless labourers as well.[1] Again, some would restrict it to tillers of the land while others would include in addition all those who live by the various forms of labour which are associated with a community of tillers.[2]

Secondly, peasants are viewed as occupying a low position in most societies. Even those who profess to admire the peasant qualities of hard work, thrift and simplicity concede that their actual rank in society is not high. The peasantry are often defined by opposition with the nobility or the gentry. 'Nobility' and 'gentry' are both terms with diverse meanings which need not be discussed here; we shall use the term 'gentry' in a very broad sense to refer to strata which live off the land but without engaging in labour. The contrast between peasantry and gentry must always be kept in mind, particularly when dealing with societies which are highly stratified.

The position of the peasantry in the order of stratification is viewed not simply in economic but also in cultural terms. Even when they own the land which they till, the holding is of small or medium size and the income from it barely sufficient to keep the family on the level of subsistence. But in addition to this, peasants are also viewed as 'rustics', i.e. persons who are untutored and unlettered. It is only the anthropologist who investigates peasant styles of life and peasant culture. In the popular meaning—which equates culture with refinement—the peasant lacks both style and culture.

The third shade of meaning derives from the language of political debate. Just as in one sense peasantry are the opposite of gentry, so also in another are peasants the counterparts of workers. The slogan 'peasants and workers' has a familiar ring in all Asian countries. This slogan draws attention to the oppression and exploitation suffered by the peasants at the hands of various classes. It assumes a clear line of demarcation between the exploited peasantry and their exploiters.

If we keep all these shades of meaning in mind we will see how

[1] See Daniel Thorner, 'Peasantry' in David L. Sils (ed.), *International Encyclopedia of the Social Sciences*, The Macmillan Company & The Free Press, 1968, Vol. 11, pp 503–11.

[2] Raymond Firth seems to prefer this broader conception; see his *Malay Fishermen, Their Peasant Economy*, Routledge and Kegan Paul, 1946.

inappropriate it is to use the blanket term 'peasant society' to characterize whole civilizations like China and India. I believe that it is inappropriate to apply this term even to the rural sector of Indian society, although it might well cover the rural sector of other societies. As to individual rural communities, they have to be investigated in detail to see what part peasants play in their social and cultural life and with what other strata they co-exist.

For purposes of scientific discussion, clearly it is not enough to limit oneself to the popular meanings of basic concepts and categories. We shall now consider briefly two of the several definitions proposed by scholars of the categories which concern us. Fortunately these do not contradict the popular conceptions with which we started but help to give them rigour and precision.

Redfield, the pioneer among anthropologists in the field of peasant studies, urged caution in the formulation of definitions. He stressed their arbitrary nature as they were designed to comprehend clusters of real societies and cultures which differed somewhat among themselves. In other words, a definition of peasants formulated primarily on the basis of European experience would reflect European reality, and must therefore be used with caution in the study of Indian society. It is worth making this point because Indian anthropologists do not appear to have pondered sufficiently on the specific characteristics of Indian peasants and have assumed that they must be the same as those of peasants everywhere.

There are two major elements in Redfield's definition of peasants. The first specifies their mode of livelihood and the second their relationship to other strata. Peasants are, to begin with, 'small producers for their own consumption'.[3] But this conception, which Redfield attributes to Firth, is too broad, for it would include Malay fishermen at one end and Sioux hunters and gatherers at the other. Hence he would like to describe as peasants only those small producers 'who make a living and have a way of life through cultivation of the land'.[4] Further, following Eric Wolf, Redfield would like to confine the term peasants to those small agriculturists who produce for their own consumption, describing as farmers those who produce for the market. He would also like to follow Wolf in limiting

[3] Robert Redfield, *Peasant Society and Culture, An Anthropological Approach to Civilization*, University of Chicago Press, 1956.
[4] Ibid., p. 18.

the term to those smallholding cultivators who control the land which they cultivate and are to that extent economically independent. When we turn to India with its elaborate tenurial arrangements we see at once the kind of problem this raises. Are tenants with occupancy rights peasants? What about sharecroppers, of whom there are several varieties even in a single state like West Bengal?

The second element in Redfield's definition places peasants in relational opposition to 'an elite of the manor, town or city'.[5] This corresponds to the opposition between peasantry and gentry to which we referred earlier. It is a significant indicator, with this important qualification that the elite or the gentry need not be 'of the manor, town or city', but may be a part of the village itself. In other words, I am arguing that the division between a lower stratum of peasants and an upper stratum of non-peasants might represent not a division between village and manor, or village and town, or village and city, but a cleavage within the village itself.

A more recent attempt to provide a definition is that of Teodor Shanin.[6] Shanin incorporates many of Redfield's ideas while adding a few others, and his definition is therefore more comprehensive. Besides the social and cultural characteristics of the peasantry, he also takes into account their political situation. But like Redfield, Shanin too tends to use the terms 'peasantry', 'peasant community' and 'peasant society' loosely and almost interchangeably.

Shanin describes what he calls peasant societies in terms of four basic facets which are as follows: '1. The peasant family farm as the basic unit of multidimensional social organization. . . . 2. Land husbandry as the main means of livelihood directly providing the major part of the consumption needs. . . . 3. Specific traditional culture related to the way of life of small communities. . . . 4. The underdog position—the domination of peasantry by outsiders'.[7] The second and third of these features do not call for any separate comment, hence I shall confine my observations to the first and the last.

The central significance of the peasant family as a unit of both consumption and production has of course been noted by many. In fact, nineteenth-century sociologists like Le Play and Tönnies would argue that the integral character of the family in work and leisure

[5] Ibid., p. 20.

[6] Teodor Shanin (ed.), *Peasants and Peasant Societies, Selected Readings*, Penguin, 1971, 'Introduction'.

[7] Ibid., pp. 14–15.

is what differentiates the peasant way of life from the industrial. However, when we define peasants in terms of the part played by the family on the farm, we must examine with some care the actual organization of work. When either the women or the men are customarily debarred from some or all forms of outdoor manual work, are we justified in describing them as peasants?

Shanin's last point, though introduced unobtrusively, represents a rather different perspective from that of Redfield. It derives from the Marxist or, more accurately, the Leninist tradition in sociology. The contrast between Redfield's and Lenin's perspectives on peasants reflects the difference between what Ossowski would describe as the 'functional' and the 'dichotomous' views of society.[8] The first view stresses the organic bonds between peasantry, gentry and other social strata while the second draws attention to the cleavage between an exploited class of peasants and their exploiters.

It is particularly interesting that in spite of this difference both Redfield and Shanin view the relationship between peasants and non-peasants as one between 'insiders' and 'outsiders'. For Redfield peasants in villages have their opposite numbers in 'the manor, town or city'; for Shanin peasants have an underdog position in which they are subjected to domination 'by outsiders'. Both seem to picture the village as the locus of a relatively homogeneous community of peasants.

The conceptual identity of village and peasant community is deeply rooted in both European scholarship and European ideology. Historians, jurists and economists writing about European countries have repeatedly characterized the village as a community of peasants. The same characterization—if anything in an even more extreme form—is found in the writings of European ideologues. The best example of this conceptual identification is to be found in the nineteenth century debate centring around the Russian *mir*, and its most forceful expression in the writings of the *narodniki*.

The writings of contemporary East European scholars from Mitrany to Georgescu-Roegen reveal the same point of view. Thus when Mitrany writes about the effects of land reforms in Rumania he treats the village and its peasants as interchangeable:[9] the village is where peasants live and those who live in the village are peasants. In a similar

[8] Stanislav Ossowski, *Class Structure in the Social Consciousness*, Routledge and Kegan Paul, 1963.

[9] David Mitrany, *The Land and the Peasant in Rumania, The War and Agrarian Reform (1917–21)*, O.U.P., 1930.

vein, in writing about 'Economic Theory and Agrarian Economics', Georgescu-Roegen equates village and peasant community.[10] He views the economic affairs of the village as being governed by rules that have a distinctive character by virtue of the intrinsic nature of peasant ways of life.

It is difficult to say how much of this identification of the village with its community of peasants in Europe is the result of an optical illusion. After all, what is highly differentiated internally often appears homogeneous at a distance. Those who wrote about village or peasant communities, whether of East or West Europe, were urban intellectuals—as Georgescu-Roegen has pointed out forcefully in regard to Marx.[11] It is not improbable that their notions about these communities should be slightly hazy and that they should invest the village with a little more homogeneity than it actually possessed. And even though the *narodniki* might have an intimate knowledge of peasant ways of life, they were clearly not writing about the Russian *mir* in the spirit of modern anthropologists.

Despite these reservations, one does have the general impression that the European village was in reality a relatively homogeneous and unstratified community. This was due in part to the manorial system which segregated the 'lord' in his manor from his 'peasants' in their village. Undoubtedly the European village varied greatly in its composition from one geographical region to another and from one historical period to the next. But social stratification was probably less a feature of the internal structure of the village than of its relation to the outside world.

It is difficult to say how far the European image of the peasant village influenced what British scholars and administrators perceived and wrote about the Indian village community before the days of intensive fieldwork. We have no reason to believe that Maine or Baden-Powell approached the Indian village without any preconceived notion of the kind of community a village would be. Nor can we say how intimate their knowledge was, judged by the standards of contemporary fieldwork, of the villages about which they wrote. They might well have approached village India with the belief, which Redfield held in more recent times, that peasants constitute 'the rural dimensions of old civilizations'.[12]

[10] N. Georgescu-Roegen, 'Economic Theory and Agrarian Economics', *Oxford Economic Papers*, Vol. 12, 1960, pp. 1–40.   [11] Ibid.

[12] Redfield, *Peasant Society and Culture*, op. cit., p. 20.

Whatever might be the true nature and composition of the European village, Redfield and Shanin have both provided useful definitions of the peasantry in which their simple and undifferentiated character is emphasized. Further, these definitions have the merit of being fairly close to the ordinary meanings of them. However, there are important sections of people in rural India—or in the Indian village —who do not fit this conception of the peasantry whichever way we look at it.

As we have seen, a peasant community, ideally conceived, is undifferentiated and unstratified. But what we learn from the many village studies now available is that the Indian village is often highly differentiated and generally stratified. This is far from saying that there are no peasants in the typical Indian village or even that there are no peasant villages in India; but it draws attention to the complex nature of rural society in India and to the varieties of villages in the country.

In order to make our argument clear we shall begin by examining an Indian village which is plainly not a community of peasants. This is an *agraharam* village which I have called Sripuram, in the Tanjore district of Tamil Nadu.[13] Although not representative in the statistical sense of the term, the *agraharam* village, of the kind exemplified by Sripuram, was by no means uncommon in this area even fifty years ago. Sounderaraja Iyengar mentions two principal kinds of villages, the *agraharavadai* dominated by Brahmins, and the *pandaravadai* dominated by the Non-Brahmins.[14] Of these the *pandaravadai* was clearly a closer approximation to the ideal type of a peasant village.

Sripuram is a large village of 349 households with a highly differentiated and stratified social structure. It is an ancient village, and its rich historical tradition is very much a part of the consciousness of at least the literate sections of its inhabitants. It has an ancient Shiva temple which bears inscriptions of the Chola kings of the eleventh century. It is, besides, a *padal sthalam*, or a place commemorated in song by the Shaiva *nayanmar* saints. In more recent times it has been associated with a disciple of the musician-saint Thyagaraja who contributed a distinctive mode of rendering classical Carnatic music named after the village.

Ninety-two of the 349 households in the village are of Brahmins,

[13] André Béteille, *Caste, Class, and Power: Changing Patterns of Stratification in a Tanjore Village*, University of California Press, 1965.

[14] S. Sounderaraja Iyengar, *Land Tenures in Madras Presidency*, Madras, 1933.

who all live in brick-and-tile houses in a separate street known as the *agraharam*. It is difficult to say how far the Brahmins of Sripuram correspond to a gentry in the European sense, but they cannot in any meaningful sense be grouped with the peasantry. They differ in almost every important respect—in food, habitation, dress and speech—from the peasants who are also a part of the village. And of course they are debarred by traditional sanctions from tilling the land which is the essential condition of the peasant's life.

The Brahmins of Sripuram and of other villages like it are known collectively as *mirasdars*. The Tanjore *mirasdar* is not only a land-owner and rentier but also a man of leisure and cultivated taste. About ten years ago an article was published about the Tanjore *mirasdar*, presumably by one of the fraternity: 'In some instances, he had read widely, especially in Sanskrit. But mostly he preferred to stroll through life. Not for him the rude contact with labour. He preferred to watch and to contemplate. Yet he was not the social parasite that this may suggest. The fact was that he was rather the connoisseur of life, tasting it at many points.'[15] Here we get a vivid, if somewhat idyllic, picture of the Brahmin *mirasdar* of Tanjore in the early part of the century.

The Brahmins of Sripuram have pursued Sanskritic learning for centuries. Indeed their ancestors were settled in the village and granted land not in order to till but so as to be able to dedicate themselves to a life of learning, teaching and ritual. There are several families in the *agraharam* whose ancestors specialized in particular branches of Sanskritic learning. Not all the Brahmins in the village or even a majority of them are conversant with Sanskrit. But they are all equally conscious of their literary and classical heritage, placing a higher value on Sanskrit than on Tamil which is the language of their speech.

There are Brahmin villages like Sripuram throughout the country from Kashmir in the north to Tamil Nadu in the south, and from West Bengal in the east to Maharashtra in the west. Not all communities of Brahmins have kept up their heritage of Sanskritic learning, and they do not all have the same degree of 'culture', to use the term in its popular meaning. But everywhere there are ritual sanctions against their tilling the land which, as we have seen, is what makes a peasant what he is.

Brahmins are not the only category of people whose traditional

[15] Published in the Madras weekly, *Swarajya*, Vol. 5, 1961, No. 46, p. 13.

style of life excluded the cultivation of land. Rajputs of proper caste and lineage were also debarred by ritual sanctions from using the plough. Further, the vast majority of Rajputs lived not in 'the manor, town or city' but in rural areas, as integral parts of village communities. Rajasthan is the state in which Rajputs are found in their most characteristic condition. Apart from the princes, *thikanedars* and *jagirdars*, there are communities of lesser Rajputs such as the *bhomias* of the Shekhawati area who have for centuries had their land cultivated by their tenants of lower caste.[16]

Some have suggested that the avoidance of ploughing and of manual work in general is based on the ritual attitudes towards purity and pollution and is therefore essentially a question of caste, but the matter is in fact more complex than that. Aristocratic and high status Muslims throughout rural India have shown an aversion for manual work which is as strong as that of the higher Hindu castes. In the villages of Burdwan district I encountered two categories of Muslims, the *ayamadar* or landlord, and *chashi* or peasant; the former kept their women in *purdah* and did not till the land. As is well known, these distinctions were even more marked in Uttar Pradesh and the former state of Hyderabad.

To come back to Sripuram, the village does not consist only of *mirasdar* Brahmins, and we must now take a look at some of the other sections of its population. The largest group of castes consists of a broad category described as Non-Brahmins and they include artisans as well as cultivators. There are three groups of 'cultivating castes' of which the principal ones are Vellalas, Kallas and Padayachis. In a broad sense it was the members of these groups who constituted the village peasantry, although they were tenants rather than owner-cultivators. Further, they were assisted, generally in the more rough and dirty work, by the Palla and Paraiya landless labourers.

In contrast to Sripuram is the village of Kila Ulur, situated in a different part of Tanjore district, described by Gilbert Étienne.[17] It seems to me that Kila Ulur may in a broad sense be described as a peasant village even though there are several different castes in it, both Non-Brahmin and Harijan, and not all its households are of owner-cultivators. More than half of its economically active popu-

[16] I am grateful for the information on the *bhomias* to Anand Chakravarti whose study of a *bhomia* village in Jaipur district is to be published soon.

[17] Gilbert Étienne, *Studies in Indian Agriculture, The Art of the Possible*, University of California Press, 1968.

lation consists of owner-cultivators and 'share-cropping is of small importance'[18] although there is a substantial population of landless labourers. Kila Ulur does not have Brahmin *mirasdars* or a separate stratum of rentiers of any other kind.

The Vellalas of Sripuram, the Kallas of Kila Ulur, the Okkaligas of Rampura and similar groups throughout the country are often described as 'cultivating' or 'peasant' castes. This blanket categorization has to be examined with care. For while the Brahmins of Tanjore and the Rajputs of Jaipur might be categorically described as non-cultivating or non-peasant castes since their traditional style of life excludes tillage, the larger castes of the middle level are too heterogeneous to be covered adequately by a blanket categorization.

When we come to castes such as the Vellalas of Tamil Nadu, the Sadgopes of West Bengal or the Marathas of Maharashtra, we have to take into account the internal differentiation and stratification that exists within each one of them. If our interest is in the agrarian social structure, then at the level of micro-analysis or of village studies we will have to treat in these cases not the caste or subcaste but the family or household as the unit of investigation and analysis. We will then probably find that some families of Vellalas (or of Sadgopes or of Marathas) are not peasants in the proper sense of the term, that others are clearly peasants and that yet others occupy a borderline position in terms of their actual role in production.

It was my experience during fieldwork in Burdwan district that some families of Sadgopes—whom I had till then viewed as a 'peasant' caste—did not participate in the actual work of tillage even when they lived in the village and owned holdings of only moderate size. They had their land cultivated either by sharecroppers or by wage labourers. I later discovered that this withdrawal from the labour force was not a matter of personal idiosyncrasy but was associated with socially-defined conceptions of status and family honour. Now when a number of related families have withdrawn from the actual work of tillage for at least two or three generations owing to discernible social causes, they have, in my view, ceased to be peasants.

If we direct our investigation to the family or household rather than the caste or subcaste, I am sure we will be able to discover numerous such cases of 'lapsed peasants' among the so-called peasant castes throughout the country. This kind of investigation is also bound to reveal a large number of borderline cases of households

[18] Ibid., p. 207.

whose status is from our point of view ambiguous. There will first of all be those families whose members have recently withdrawn from the labour force. They either give their land out to sharecroppers or have it tilled by wage labourers, engaging occasionally in actual farm work, and in other ways continuing to pursue a peasant style of life.

A more important factor behind this kind of ambiguity relates to the position of women in Indian society. As noted earlier, a peasant household in the true sense is one in which all its active members, both men and women, work on the farm. How are we to view families in which men work in the fields but women are by custom debarred from such work? Are these to be viewed as families of peasants or are they not? This question acquires particular importance in those forms of agriculture, such as wet paddy cultivation, which are based on an elaborate sexwise division of labour and in which the work cannot be completed without the participation of women. Sir Denzil Ibbetson's comment, 'The Jat calls himself *zamindar* or "husbandman' as often as Jat, and his women and children alike work with him in the fields'[19] may or may not hold for all Jat agriculturists, but it certainly does not hold for all families believed to be of peasant caste.

We have little precise information about the work done by women outside the home in the different strata of society in rural India. To the extent that we talk at all systematically about the organization of work in agriculture, we do so almost entirely from the man's point of view. This is unfortunate particularly because in India what women may or may not do is often a more sensitive indicator of family status than what is permitted or practised among men. It seems reasonable to maintain that a family of non-cultivating landowners moves down one step on the social ladder when its men go to work in the fields, but it comes down several steps when its women have to do the same. And if this is true of Hindus, it is even more true of Muslims.

The whole process of status mobility, or what Srinivas describes as Sanskritization, can be examined in this light. When a family of proper peasants which has improved its economic position wishes

[19] Cited in *Panjab Castes, Being a reprint of the chapter on 'The Races, Castes, and Tribes of the People' in the Report on the Census of the Punjab published in 1883 by the late Sir Denzil Ibbetson, K. C. S. I.*, Languages Department, Panjab, 1970, p. 103.

to move up socially, it first withdraws its women from agriculture and then its men. One may even be able to trace out a regular sequence of steps. Women are first withdrawn from wage employment on the farms of others. They are then withdrawn from the family farm. Finally, the men either withdraw from work or change their role from cultivator to supervisor.

The role of women in Indian agriculture is particularly noteworthy because in this regard India seems to differ radically from the other major agrarian society, China. I am not referring here to China after the Communist revolution, which has evidently brought about great changes in the relations between the sexes, but about conditions in pre-Communist China. Admittedly our material on agricultural communities in traditional China is very limited, and our observations on this question must be made with caution and remain provisional. But whatever evidence we have seems to suggest that women played a much more active role on the family farm over a much wider range of the system of stratification in China than in India.

The few village studies that we have from China by Chinese anthropologists show that both men and women work actively on the farm. It is not as if these communities are totally unstratified, but such stratification as there is within the village does not take the form of a structural cleavage between families whose members work for themselves and others, and families for whom others work. In fact persons from even fairly prosperous families might work for wages for others who are less prosperous than they: these are proper communities of peasants.

It is not as if people never withdraw from farm work after becoming economically prosperous. But what Fei tells us is that in China it is the men who first withdraw in such cases, leaving the women to continue to work on the farm. 'The statement made previously that there is a tendency for landowners to avoid working on their farms might seem to be contradicted by the fact that women of all families, even those with large landholdings, are invariably active in agriculture. During the harvest period almost every woman in the village, except those occupied in cooking for the workers, is to be found toiling in the fields, while the little girls who are too young for farm work care for the babies.'[20]

[20] Fei Hsiao-Tung and Chang Chih-I, *Earthbound China, A Study of Rural Economy in Yunnan*, Routledge and Kegan Paul, 1949, p. 65.

Fei goes on to describe the case of a particular landowner who lived a life of leisure but had 'a pretty young daughter who could be found working in the fields, either on her father's or on some other farm, almost any day in the busy season.'[21] These observations appear so startling to a student of Indian society that he might doubt their authenticity had they not been supported by the authority of Fei Hsiao-Tung.

It is clear that Fei is not describing something accidental or peculiar to a particular village, for he has a theory to account for the unequal contribution of men and women to agricultural work. 'In the earlier discussion on farm labour I emphasized the fact that even in the very wealthy houses the women and girls work regularly in the fields. Although it may not seem fair that the weaker sex, with their bound feet, should toil in the mud while the men spend their days in idleness, an examination of property structure of the family makes it appear that there is a kind of balance and reciprocity in the household economy.'[22]

The argument, briefly speaking, is that since men (and not women) own the land, it is they who decide, naturally to their own advantage, who should be exempted from toil.

Fei's theory is not very satisfactory. Men own the land in India also, and presumably in India also it is they who decide which members of the family will be withdrawn from agricultural work in which order. But in this country it is the women and not the men who are the first to be withdrawn, and among wealthy, high status families there is never any question of women going out to work for wages on other people's land.

In reality the role of women in agriculture and the division of work in the peasant family as a whole are governed not merely by the structure of property rights, but also by a variety of conceptions such as those of status, honour and purity. These conceptions are culturally specific which means that they differ in their scope and significance from one society to another, and in the same society from one stratum to another. If we are to study peasant households or peasant communities in a more meaningful way, we will have to devote more serious attention to these beliefs, values and sentiments, particularly when we are comparing one society with another.

The purity of women in Hindu society is a subject in itself, and it has been discussed elaborately and at length in the context of marriage

[21] Ibid., p. 66.   [22] Ibid., p. 111.

5

rules and practices.[23] It has not been discussed so far by sociologists in a systematic way in the context of extra-domestic work, particularly the type of work which involves the joint participation of men and women. It is generally known that the concepts of purity and pollution debar members of certain castes from tilling the land while allowing others to do it. We are likely to get a more differentiated picture of the domestic economy if we remember that the concepts of purity and pollution apply differently to men and to women.

If the concept of ritual purity is specific to Hinduism, that of social honour is more general, applying to both Hindus and Muslims, though perhaps in somewhat different ways. The institution of *purdah* has for centuries been the hallmark of status among Muslims in India, and among poorer Muslims of aristocratic pretensions it has been and continues to be a severe strain on the economic resources of the family. Among the Hindus, similar considerations govern the Rajput style of life, and, as is well known, families with claims to Rajput status are a common feature of the entire Hindi-speaking region.

We have come a long way from the facile assumption that all those who live in villages, men and women, may be described as peasants. The population of the Indian village is often highly stratified and some of these strata are clearly different from peasants in any sense of the term. While we do get a broad notion of this order of stratification from a consideration of caste, this is not enough. In order to get a more accurate picture, particularly of groups at the middle of the hierarchy, we have to take the family as the unit and to examine in particular the division of work between men and women within and outside the domestic sphere.

There are different types of villages in India. Some clearly are peasant villages, whereas in others non-peasants co-exist with peasants and may even predominate over them, if not in numbers at least in social, economic and political influence. It is possible that villages of different types predominate in different regions, although each major region will have several types of villages.

The point which I would like to emphasize in conclusion is the co-existence of 'peasantry' and 'gentry' as a common feature of many Indian villages and a characteristic feature of some. This is at

[23] Nur Yalman, 'On the Purity of Women in the Castes of Ceylon and Malabar', *Journal of the Royal Anthropological Institute*, Vol. 93, Part 1, 1963, pp. 25–8.

variance with the European conception of the village and perhaps also the European reality. But in order to be able to say anything with confidence on this question we need a much fuller investigation of the facts. It is my belief that the vague and imprecise concept of 'peasant society', which has gained currency among sociologists and social anthropologists, stands as an obstacle in the way of this kind of investigation.

The most interesting comparison is not between India and Europe, but between India and China. We have already seen that there are certain differences between these two major Asian countries in their traditional productive organizations. The attitudes towards the place of women on the farm are clearly different in the two countries, if we can go by Fei's testimony and our own observations. Further, all the villages studied by Chinese anthropologists are or closely approximate to peasant communities whereas this is by no means the case in India, although this difference may be partly due to the criteria adopted in the selection of the two sets of villages.

The apparent predominance of peasant villages in China may be related to a significant observation made by Fei. In a discussion of peasantry and gentry in China, Fei maintains that there is not only a social but an ecological separation between the two. He remarks, 'The peasantry and gentry can further be contrasted by showing their ecological positions.'[24] There is little scope for peasants to improve their economic position within the village. 'Therefore, it is essential for the rich to keep away from the village. The place where they can maintain their power and wealth is the town.'[25] While towns have certainly been important centres of civilization in India, there has always been ample scope within the village itself for the rich to maintain their power and wealth.

[24] Fei Hsiao-Tung, 'Peasantry and Gentry in China, An Interpretation of Chinese Social Structure and its Changes' in Reinhard Bendix and Seymour Martin Lipset (eds.), *Class, Status and Power, A Reader in Social Stratification*, Routledge and Kegan Paul, 1954, p. 637.
[25] Ibid.

4

Tribe and Peasantry

A NUMBER OF different streams of scholarship have contributed to the study of peasants. Historians, economists and social anthropologists have enriched our knowledge of peasant social structure and culture in various ways. One may observe certain differences in the characterization of the peasantry offered by scholars pursuing these different disciplines. This is partly, and at least on the surface, due to differences in the empirical material on which they have worked. But it is no less due to differences in the conceptual schemes and theoretical questions which they have brought to the study of the peasantry from their respective disciplines.

In this chapter the contribution made to peasant studies primarily by the anthropological stream will be examined. The most notable feature of this contribution lies in the richness of the empirical material it brought into the analysis of the peasantry. This empirical material was not only very rich, but was of an altogether new kind. Here were scholars who were for the first time studying peasants by living among them, and examining systematically and in detail the various facets of peasant life as it was actually lived.

However, we must not forget that anthropologists had first specialized in the study of tribes before they undertook the study of peasants. Their stock of theories, concepts and methods had acquired shape in the course of their studies of primitive, pre-literate or tribal communities, and it was only natural that these should influence to some extent not only their investigation of peasant communities, but also their characterization of them. Hence in order to understand how anthropologists came to view peasants we must know a little about how they had earlier come to view tribes.

The first anthropological studies of village communities in complex societies were viewed outside the profession with some misgiving if not suspicion. I was told by a distinguished Japanese scholar that the weakness of Embree's study of Suye Mura[1] was that it made the Japanese village appear like a primitive tribal community. The burden of this kind of criticism is that the internal structure of a Japanese village (or an Indian village) has an order of complexity which is quite different from what one encounters in a tribal community.

It is not that anthropologists were unaccustomed to dealing with complex structural problems, but their work in tribal societies had trained them to seek out only some and not all types of complexity. To be specific, anthropologists were highly skilled at identifying and analysing kinship and lineage structures, but on the whole somewhat inept at handling class and social stratification. For this reason they often ignored or paid insufficient attention to the structure of inequalities, at least in their earlier village studies. As a consequence, villages of very different kinds all came to be regarded as communities of peasants. The resulting ambiguity can be easily seen in the anthropological literature on the peasantry. We are told, for instance, that 'the peasant village is heterogeneous in terms of internal division into caste and class'.[2] It is unlikely that an economist or a historian who is used to viewing peasants as a class or a stratum would write in this way. For if the peasants are treated as a particular class, then the term 'peasant' cannot be applied to a community which is internally divided into diverse classes.

But this represents only one side of the coin. For if anthropologists have implicitly viewed peasant communities in terms of tribal categories, they have also been unusually keen to distinguish explicitly between 'tribe' and 'peasant'. One can go even further and say that if there is something distinctive in the anthropologist's characterization of the peasantry, it derives from the way in which he contrasts the two sociological types. The economist or historian on the other hand has not viewed 'tribe' and 'peasant' as mutually exclusive categories.

If one were to approach the study of the peasantry as an economic historian, one might characterize peasants by contrasting them not with tribesmen but with the other classes or strata in a complex

[1] John F. Embree, *A Japanese Village: Suye Mura*, Routledge and Kegan Paul, 1946.
[2] Surajit Sinha, 'Tribe-Caste and Tribe-Peasant Continua in Central India', *Man in India*, Vol. 45, No. 1, 1965, p. 62.

society. It is not that social anthropologists have completely ignored the relationship between peasants and other social strata. Redfield, for instance, saw the importance of the distinction between peasantry and gentry within the framework of a complex society. But in defining the characteristics of what he called peasant society he placed much greater emphasis on its contrast with tribal society.[3]

There is clearly a difference between contrasting peasants with tribesmen and contrasting peasantry with gentry. In the first case we are, as it were, contrasting two different types of society whereas in the second we are contrasting two strata within the same society. It can be shown that many anthropologists talk about tribe and peasant as though they constituted different societies. This creates problems when we are dealing with societies of the Indian kind where tribes, peasantry and gentry constitute elements within one and the same society.

It has to be admitted that there is something basically unsatisfactory about the scheme adopted by Redfield and his followers which divides Indian society into three sectors, tribal, peasant and urban.[4] The three terms in the scheme are logically disparate. Clearly, one can think of an alternative scheme in which the three terms would be tribesmen, peasantry and gentry. One might then find that the difference between tribesmen and peasants in India is in general much smaller than the difference between either of them and the gentry.

It is no doubt possible to use the labels 'tribal' and 'peasant' for two types of social organization and to characterize one by contrasting it with the other. But in spite of all the effort invested by anthropologists in the study of primitive societies, there really is no satisfactory way of defining a tribal society. What this amounts to in the Indian context is that anthropologists have tried to characterize a somewhat nebulous sociological type by contrasting it with another which is almost equally nebulous. Earlier anthropologists had not paid sufficient attention to the definition of tribal society, but tacitly assumed that what they were studying in Australia, Melanesia and Africa were various forms of tribal society. The tribe was somewhat

[3] Robert Redfield, *Peasant Society and Culture*, University of Chicago Press, 1956.

[4] This scheme was adopted at a seminar organized in Chicago by Robert Redfield, Milton Singer and Surajit Sinha under the auspices of the Ford Foundation in 1956.

vaguely assumed to be a more or less homogeneous society having a common government, a common dialect and a common culture. Since Evans-Pritchard's time[5] anthropologists have tried in a much more systematic way to provide a structural definition of the tribe, particularly in the context of segmentary societies.

However, as I. M. Lewis indicates, it is one thing to show how boundaries should be drawn between different tribes, and another to specify the characteristics of tribal societies as such. Lewis himself proposes the criterion of 'scale', introduced into anthropology by Godfrey and Monica Wilson,[6] to define the nature of societies of this kind. 'Ideally, tribal societies are small in scale, are restricted in the spatial and temporal range of their social, legal and political relations, and possess a morality, religion and world view of corresponding dimensions.'[7] Two comments may be made on this. Firstly, some of the major Indian tribes such as the Santals, Gonds and Bhils are quite large, numbering over a million persons each and scattered over extensive territories. Secondly, if we are considering not the tribe as a whole but 'tribal' communities, it can be shown that there are 'peasant' communities in many parts of the world which are also 'small in scale'.

A rather more interesting characterization of tribal society is the one provided by Sahlins[8] which can be traced back to the writings of scholars such as Durkheim and Mauss.[9] Sahlins has argued that the term 'tribal society' be restricted to what are called segmentary systems. Segmentary systems are not only small in scale but represent a definite structural type which is quite different from the more complex social systems in which peasantry and gentry coexist. If we define 'tribe' in this sense we will find that the Santals, Oraons and Mundas correspond less to tribes than to what are broadly described as peasants.

There is thus no one way of defining tribal society. Definitions may be either very broad and loose or very narrow and restricted. The former would apply not only to tribes but in many ways also to the

[5] E. E. Evans-Pritchard, *The Nuer*, Clarendon Press, 1940.

[6] Godfrey and Monica Wilson, *The Analysis of Social Change*, Cambridge University Press, 1945.

[7] I. M. Lewis, 'Tribal Society' in David L. Sils (ed.), *International Encyclopedia of the Social Sciences*, The Macmillan Company and The Free Press, 1968, Vol. 16, p. 147.

[8] Marshall D. Sahlins, *Tribesmen*, Prentice-Hall, 1968.

[9] See Marcel Mauss, *Oeuvres*, Vol. III, Les Editions de Minuit, 1969, pp. 580 ff.

peasantry. The latter would exclude many societies which have been conventionally regarded as tribal. It will no doubt be argued that the definition of a tribal society as a segmentary system will not be of much practical use in a country like India where segmentary societies cannot be easily identified. Bailey is perhaps the only anthropologist working in the Indian field who has tried to characterize tribes in terms of segmentary principles, but the contrast in which he is interested is not between 'tribe' and 'peasant' but between 'tribe' and 'caste'.[10]

Unlike Bailey, the majority of Indian anthropologists have not given much serious thought to the problem of creating a definition of of tribal society which will be appropriate to the Indian context. Rather they appear to have wavered continually between textbook definitions of 'tribe' and prevailing classifications of Indian society into 'tribal' and 'non-tribal'. Even if we are not able to settle once and for all what we must mean by 'tribal society' or how the term ought to be used in India, it should be worthwhile to examine the context of its use in Indian society.

The convention to categorize certain groups in Indian society as tribal was established during the nineteenth century largely by British administrators. From the 1930's onwards lists began to be prepared of Indian tribes with a view to giving them administrative and political concessions. The list of Scheduled Tribes attached to the Constitution of India had its origins in these. It cannot be too strongly emphasized that the list reflects the demands more of administrative and political circumstance than of academic or logical rigour. As a consequence the same groups might be treated as a tribe in one state but not in another. It is not surprising that Government should have a list of this kind in the interest of practical policy. What is surprising is that since independence anthropologists have more or less accepted the list without critically examining its rationale.

A notable feature of British administration in India was the task assigned to the decennial census operations. This included not only the counting of heads but the classification of the population into various categories. The successive census operations resulted in the creation of an enormously complex system of categories for dividing the population into tribes, castes, sects and occupations. Several of the earlier officials in charge of census operations were men with a

---

[10] F. G. Bailey, ' "Tribe" and "Caste" in India', *Contributions to Indian Sociology*, No. V, 1961, pp. 7–19.

passion for ethnology, and this no doubt contributed to the complexity of the categorical apparatus they created.[11]

Since our existing list of tribes derives largely from the work of these census officials, it would be only fair to say that they were not much concerned with the distinction between 'tribe' and 'peasant'. Initially they used the term 'tribe' in a rather loose sense, using it frequently to describe groups such as the Jats and Ahirs. But by the time of the 1931 census, of which J. H. Hutton was in over-all charge, the distinction between 'tribe' and 'caste' had become an issue of some importance. Tribes came to be viewed more and more in religious and not just ecological terms. If a group could be shown to be clearly 'Hindu' in its religious beliefs and practices, it was a caste; if it was 'Animist' it had to be treated as a tribe.

It is erroneous to argue that 'Animists' cannot be peasants. For by doing so the word 'peasant' would be given a very peculiar meaning. Hence for the time being we should set aside altogether the scheme which divides Indian society into tribal, peasant and urban, and examine to what extent and in what sense our tribal people can also be regarded as peasants.

India has probably the largest tribal population of any country in the world, if we go by the official classification. Apart from the large size of this population—over thirty million in 1971—its most striking feature is its enormous diversity. The tribal people are to be found in various parts of the country, although there are large concentrations of them in particular regions. One of the notable features of this distribution, which represents an ancient pattern, is that at least outwardly the tribal people of one particular region often resemble more closely the non-tribal people of that region than the tribal people of another region.

There is no single way of making a satisfactory classification of the 427 tribes found in India. I propose to follow here the classification adopted by N. K. Bose. 'There are many ways in which tribes can be classified. One, as we have already said, is by language; another is by religion; a third is by the degree of isolation to which they are subject, which has led some to retain a larger proportion of their original culture than others. But, we believe, the plainest way will be to arrange them into categories based on the manner in which they

[11] R. Saumerez Smith, *Caste, Religion and Locality in the Punjab Census*, M. Litt. dissertation submitted to the University of Delhi, 1971.

primarily make their living.'[12] For a discussion which seeks to inquire whether tribes can also be regarded as peasants, this is obviously the most satisfactory procedure. Bose divides the tribal people into three principal categories, (i) hunters, fishers and gatherers; (ii) shifting cultivators; and (iii) settled agriculturists using the plough and plough cattle. He lists two other categories, viz. nomadic cattle keepers, artisans and labourers; and workers in plantations and industries. Among these it is the settled agriculturists using the plough and plough cattle who account for the overwhelming majority of the tribal people; the workers in plantations and industries are also recruited mainly from their ranks.

The larger tribes which number over a million persons each—the Santals, Gonds, Bhils, Oraons and Mundas—are all settled agriculturists and have been so for generations. Their members are today 'classified under the categories of cultivators, agricultural labourers and workers in certain other primary types of occupation'.[13] Bose has revealed the presence of a simple but definite division of labour in their villages. Thus one can find in these tribal villages, in addition to cultivators, households specializing in such crafts as basket-making, oil-pressing and blacksmithery—all necessary elements in an economy of land and grain.

My first exposure as a fieldworker to the tribal people of India was in Ranchi district where I made observations in an Oraon village in 1956-7. Later I was able to observe Santal villages in Hazaribagh district in the course of a survey made under the auspices of the Indian Statistical Institute. Although these exposures were brief and I spent just a month studying material culture, social organization and religion in an Oraon village in Ranchi district, I came away with the strong impression that the inhabitants of these villages corresponded very closely to the ordinary meaning of peasants. I clearly remember my initial disappointment in discovering that, although we had come to investigate proper tribals, the people who confronted us were outwardly no different from the poorer villagers one might find anywhere in rural Bihar or West Bengal. The Oraon inhabitants of the village in Ranchi district which I had investigated fit very well into Shanin's conception of the peasantry discussed in the previous chapter.[14] It seems to me that they fit this conception much better

[12] N. K. Bose, *Tribal Life in India*, New Delhi, 1971, pp. 4–5. [13] Ibid. p. 23.
[14] Teodor Shanin (ed.), *Peasants and Peasant Societies*, Penguin, 1971, Introduction.

than the people of the village in Tanjore district I investigated five years later. It will be useful to take up the main points in Shanin's conception and see in a general way whether they apply to the inhabitants of the Oraon, Munda, Ho and Santal villages of Chota Nagpur.

The first characteristic of the peasantry is the central importance of the family farm. Although the clan and the lineage have been, and continue to be, important structural units among the agricultural tribes of Chota Nagpur, it is really the family which is the principal unit of both production and consumption. Individual families act as units of production on land which they themselves control (as 'cultivators') or on land owned and controlled by others (as sharecroppers or agricultural labourers). In either case both men and women participate jointly in agricultural work, contrary to the practice of high status families among Hindus and Muslims, including families belonging to the so-called cultivating castes.

Secondly, not only do these families engage in settled agriculture but land husbandry constitutes for them the main means of livelihood and provides for the major part of their consumption needs. Almost all these tribes have myths which speak of an earlier phase when they lived by hunting and gathering and which make a symbolic assertion of the place of these activities in their culture. But it is difficult to translate these myths into historical terms, and clearly these tribes have lived by settled agriculture for at least five generations and probably longer. Further, their agriculture has been primarily a subsistence agriculture, although it may be rash to assert that they have had no links with markets.

The third point in Shanin's characterization of the peasantry is about their 'specific traditional culture related to the way of life of small communities'.[15] What Shanin has in mind are features such as conformity to age-old habits and practices and the subordination of the individual to the community. As he rightly points out, these follow more or less from life in fairly small and stable local communities. Once again, if we were to look for these features in rural India, the Santal, Oraon or Munda village would be a good place in which to begin.

Finally, we have what Shanin calls the 'underdog position' of the peasantry, or their domination by outsiders. Peasants occupy, as it were by definition, a subordinate position in all stratified societies, but the extent of their exploitation varies greatly from one society to

[15] Ibid., p. 15.

another, and within the same society from one region to another. I have argued that peasants are not necessarily exploited by 'outsiders'; their exploiters in the highly-stratified Indian village are often other strata of the village itself. But if there is any single category of Indian peasants who have been exploited from 'outside' for over a century, it is the Oraon, Munda and Santal villagers of Chota Nagpur, and tribal agriculturists in India as a whole.

One important reason why the exploiters of these tillers of the land—moneylenders, revenue farmers, landlords—are mainly out-siders is that the Santal, Oraon, Ho or Munda village is itself relatively homogeneous and unstratified. It is, above all, in this sense that these villages are to be viewed as true communities of peasants. Economic inequalities no doubt exist in these villages, but they are of a totally different order from the inequalities present in villages where Brahmin or Rajput or Muslim landlords reside.

Our general impression of the peasant economy of the larger tribes of Chota Nagpur has of course to be tested by a detailed and system-atic examination of the facts. This is particularly necessary if we are to avoid making general statements about tribes which will be as vast and empty as the ones about peasants we commented upon in the previous chapter. India has a large number of tribes which, as we saw earlier, differ very much from each other, and while some correspond to peasants, others do not. What is more important is that a single 'tribe' such as the Bhil or the Gond sometimes turns out to be an aggregate of many sections, some clearly being peasants and others, equally clearly, being not.

Unfortunately, detailed studies of tribal communities in their tradi-tional context are no longer made as widely as in the past. The trend in the last two decades has been to replace tribal monographs with 'village studies'. What is remarkable about this shift in interest among Indian anthropologists is that 'village studies' are viewed as different from or alternative to 'tribal studies', whereas in fact one could very well make studies of 'tribal' villages just as studies of non-tribal villages are made. There is little doubt that this way of contrasting 'tribal studies' with 'village studies' is a direct consequence of the false opposition between 'tribe' and 'peasant' which was imposed on Indian anthropology in the middle fifties.

It is difficult to account satisfactorily for the decline of interest among anthropologists in the study of tribal communities. During the last two decades barely half-a-dozen good monographs have appeared on Indian tribes, and even these are not all studies of tribes in their 'natural' setting. It is quite understandable that so much attention should be devoted to the study of peasants by Indian anthropologists. But there is no reason why this should be done at the expense of tribal studies, particularly when so many of India's tribal communities are in fact communities of peasants.

In the absence of good recent studies on the social and economic life of the cultivating tribes, we have to go back to the monographs published by earlier scholars from S. C. Roy to C. von Fürer-Haimendorf. Unfortunately those monographs were written before the strategy of intensive village studies came to be commonly adopted by anthropologists. Most of them provide generalized accounts of the materials traits, social institutions and religious practices of the various tribes. Few of them give us the kind of detailed information, at the level of the local community, that we have for the non-tribal people in our rural areas. One of the interesting aspects of these earlier monographs is that they appear not to view 'tribe' and 'peasant' as mutually exclusive categories. S. C. Roy speaks freely of the Oraon and Munda villagers as peasants, and Fürer-Haimendorf describes the 'peasant' culture of the Raj Gonds of Adilabad. In more recent times Bailey has characterized the Konds of Orissa as peasants.

S. C. Roy's account of the Oraons, published nearly sixty years ago, provides valuable data on agriculture from the viewpoint of both material culture and social organization. Although we are not presented with a detailed description of any particular village, there is much information on the nature of village organization, including the organization of economic life. The village economy of the Oraons is essentially an economy of land and grain, although ancillary occupations are also practised by both Oraon and non-Oraon inhabitants of the village. The principal crop grown by the Oraons is paddy, although two varieties of millets, *gondli* and *marua*, are also grown and form an important ingredient in the diet of the poorer Oraons. Paddy cultivation is technologically a very complex process. Roy gives us detailed descriptions of the various operations involved— manuring, ploughing, regulation of water, sowing, transplanting, weeding, harvesting[16]—which are similar even on points of detail to the operations performed by non-tribal peasants in the plains of Bihar and West Bengal. Roy also gives us an account of the division

[16] Sarat Chandra Roy, *The Oraons of Chota Nagpur*, Ranchi, 1915, pp. 123–8.

of labour between men and women in Oraon agriculture. Women do the transplanting and weeding, men do the hoeing, ploughing, levelling and sowing while harvesting is done by both men and women;[17] here again there is a detailed similarity between Oraon agriculture and the agriculture of non-tribal peasants.

Roy's description of the composition of an Oraon village deserves to be quoted at length. 'A typical Oraon village thus consists of the Bhuinhars, subsequent Oraon settlers (called Jeth-raiyats or ordinary raiyats, according as they are earlier or later settlers) and a Gorait family, one or two Ahir families, a Lohra family, and sometimes also a family of Kumhars. In many villages, a few families of Ghasis, Jolahas or in some cases Chik Baraiks (weavers), and Mahalis (basket-makers) and a few other castes and tribes are also met with.'[18] There are two points in this description which should be particularly noted: (i) the differentiation of Oraons according to their tenurial status and (ii) the presence of both Hindu and Muslim groups of artisans.

The core of the Oraon village, according to Roy, consists of the Bhuinhars whom he characterizes as 'peasant proprietors'.[19] He believes that there was a stage in the past when these peasant proprietors were fully independent, without 'landlords over their heads', and without 'rents or taxes to pay'.[20] We do not have good historical material to be able to say when, if at all, such a condition prevailed. But by the time Roy started his investigation of the Oraons at the beginning of the twentieth century there were already among them various categories of *raiyats*, a term used throughout India to characterize cultivators or peasants. That the Oraon village at the turn of the century was not a simple tribal community is confirmed by the regular presence in it of members of various endogamous groups. The identity of these is not always easy to establish, and perhaps it is not very pertinent to ask whether groups such as the Mahalis, Ghasis and Lohras are Hinduized tribals or tribalized Hindus. From our point of view, their presence contributed just that much of heterogeneity and stratification which seems to be a characteristic feature of peasant communities throughout the world.

The Mundas of Chota Nagpur are generally believed to be older inhabitants of the area than the Oraons and to be agriculturally somewhat more backward. Nevertheless, they also have an economic system and a village organization which are basically similar to those

---

[17] Ibid., p. 131.   [18] Ibid., pp. 110–11.
[19] Ibid., p. 109.   [20] Ibid.

of the Oraons. They are settled cultivators, having a characteristically peasant division of labour within the family, and they live in
villages along with artisans who supply their basic non-agricultural
requirements.

Some interest has centred around what is known as the *khuntkatti*
tenure among the Mundas, and a brief description of the *khuntkatti*
village as it was seen at the beginning of the twentieth century would
be useful. In a special contribution to the *Encyclopaedia Mundarica*,
Hoffman and Lister write: 'The pure Mundari *khuntkatti* village
usually contains three elements, namely (a) the *khuntkattidars*, (b) the
parjas or raiyats, and (c) the subsidiary castes. The *khuntkattidars*
are the descendants in the male line of the original founders of the
village. . . The *parjas* are almost invariably Mundaris, and very often
are relatives on the female side of the *khuntkattidars*. . . . The subsidiary castes (Penrains, Mahilis or Khangars, Bhogtas, and Barais)
perform the non-agricultural functions necessary to the village life
and rarely cultivate land.'[21] The authors of the article hasten to add
that pure *khuntkatti* villages are becoming scarce and proceed to give
a description of what they call 'broken *khuntkatti* villages'. The
breakdown of *khuntkatti* villages has been associated with two
factors: (i) the emergence of individual ownership of land as opposed
to control by the local lineage and (ii) the encroachment of moneylenders and landlords into the Munda country. We do not know how
effective the control of the lineage was over the holdings operated by
particular families, and exactly when this control began to loosen.
Nor is it true that landlords and moneylenders were completely
unknown in the area before the advent of British rule.

Fürer-Haimendorf's study of the Raj Gonds of Adilabad relates
to a more recent period. Although this is a different area from Chota
Nagpur, we note here also the same three elements in the population:
(i) 'the so-called "aboriginals" ', divided into various endogamous
groups and living mainly by agriculture, (ii) 'the associated castes of
bards, musicians and craftsmen', and (iii) castes of Telugu and
Marathi extraction, and Muslims who have come mainly from outside.[22] While there is some amount of ecological separation between

[21] J. Hoffmann and E. Lister, 'Special Memorandum on the Land System of
the Munda Country' in J. Hoffmann (in collaboration with A. van Emelen),
Encyclopaedia Mundarica, Vol. VIII, Patna, 1950, p. 2389.

[22] C. von Fürer-Haimendorf (in collaboration with E. von Fürer-Haimendorf),
The Raj Gonds of Adilabad, A Peasant Culture of the Deccan, Book I, MacMillan
and Co., 1948, p. 31.

the three categories of people, villages in which the Raj Gonds live are also frequently inhabited by members of the second category. Fürer-Haimendorf takes care to point out that in Adilabad district 'the Raj Gonds do not form a ruling class or even a class of privileged economic status, but an entire tribal group comprising all strata of society from the feudal chiefs down to the poorest labourer'.[23] The Raj Gonds are jealous of their cultural identity which they seek to protect in various ways. But this form of syncretic unity—we may call it tribal identity if we wish—does not negate the diacritical unity which the Raj Gond cultivators share with cultivators belonging to other groups in the area.

We know of various types of economic systems among the Raj Gonds in terms of both technology and social organization. Shifting cultivation was widely practised in the area in earlier times and was common even in the forties. But in addition to millets, the Raj Gonds were also growing wheat and cotton. These tribal people are not only peasants but they are peasants who are now becoming increasingly articulated with a market economy.

One way of meeting my argument would be to say that while it is true that a substantial number of tribal people are peasants today, this is because we no longer have tribes in their pure state but only tribes in transition. The notion of the Indian tribes being in a state of transition was raised for systematic inquiry by Professor D. N. Majumdar nearly forty years ago.[24] Since then it has become a kind of stock-in-trade for most anthropologists writing about the tribal situation in India. There can be no question but that major changes have been taking place among India's tribal people in the course of the last hundred years. Their isolation has broken down or been reduced. In many areas shifting cultivators have become settled agriculturists using the plough and plough cattle. With changes in technology there have come about corresponding changes in their organization of production. Patterns of landholding have changed. The lineage is less important as a corporate group than it was in the past, and the market economy is altering not only the relationship of the tribal village with the outside world but also the economic and social structure of the village itself.

Unfortunately, the notion of 'transition' is in sociology a rather

[23] Ibid., p. 5.
[24] D. N. Majumdar, *A Tribe in Transition, A Study in Culture Pattern*, Longmans, 1937.

elusive one, and it is used as often to evade an argument as to confirm it. The more closely we look into the social institutions of the tribes like the Oraons, Mundas and Santhals, the more we are likely to find that they have been in transition for a period which is to be measured not in decades but in centuries. Reliable historical material on these tribes does not go very far back in time, and in any case the conditions under which their history comes to be recorded are precisely those which are associated with a transition in their life.

N. K. Bose writes about the Mundas: 'It is not unlikely that in the past the Kol or Munda tribe practised some form of slash-and-burn agriculture. Even now one might find among them vague memories of the forest being gradually cleared by burning or *jara*.'[25] However, Bose does not fail to point out that 'our earliest records of the Mundas show them as settled in permanent villages and practising plough cultivation in the uplands'.[26] These records go back to the end of the eighteenth century. Bose shows how the traditional *khuntkatti* village had begun to disintegrate during the period of Muslim rule. If the Mundas had ever been, in S. C. Roy's phrase, 'peasant proprietors' at some stage, their independence had begun to be whittled down with the emergence of a state structure in the seventeenth century itself. 'In order to enhance the splendour of the Chota Nagpur court, the king began to adorn it with Kshatriya and Brahmin attendants with titles such as *rautiya, bhaiya, brittiya, pandeya, jamadar, wohdar*, etc., and a new economic arrangement was started, based on the *jagir* system which was introduced for the maintenance of these immigrant courtiers. The oldest document recovered from the royal treasury is dated 1676.'[27]

In other words, what some would call the 'underdog position' of the Munda peasantry, or their 'exploitation by outsiders' is at least three hundred years old.

This chapter began by arguing that in the Indian context it does not seem justifiable to define 'tribe' in opposition to 'peasant' since a substantial number of tribal people are in fact peasants and have been so for a long time. Further, the accepted meaning of the phrase does not require that peasants should adhere to any particular religion; in other words, peasants may be Muslim, Christian, Hindu or

[25] Nirmal Kumar Bose, *Hindu Samajer Garhan*, Vishwabharati Granthalaya, 1356 (Bengali calendar), p. 19.
[26] Ibid., p. 18.   [27] Ibid., p. 24.

Animist. This brings us to our final question, which is whether the tribal people mentioned earlier can also be regarded as Hindus. Putting it a little differently, even if it is true that the Santals, Mundas and Oraons are peasants, one might ask if there are not substantial differences between them and the other Indian peasants who are clearly Hindus.

I would like to make it clear that the true object of sociology is not to impose a kind of unity on social phenomena, but to seek, at one and the same time, both similarities and differences among them. My purpose in drawing attention to the 'tribal' peasantry is not to establish an identity between them and the non-tribal peasantry, but to argue that the similarities between, say, Bhumij and Kurmi peasants in the economic and political spheres is probably much greater than the similarities between either and, say, Brahmin or Rajput landlords.

Hence, even if we dismiss the contrast between tribe and peasant as being largely misleading in the Indian context, we are still left with the contrast between tribe and caste. Anthropologists have differed sharply on this question. Ghurye has been of the opinion that the tribal people are 'backward Hindus', differing only in degree from the other segments of Hindu society.[28] Elwin, on the other hand, has argued forcefully and eloquently for the recognition of the separate social and cultural identity of the tribal people.[29] The Government of India, it must be noted, gives tacit recognition to this identity by keeping alive under Constitutional sanction its list of Scheduled Tribes.

There are certain commonly-observed differences between tribes and castes which may be considered briefly. There is first the relative isolation of tribes as compared with castes. This has two facets. It means, first, that the tribes are geographically isolated, being concentrated in areas which are or have been more or less inaccessible. It also means—and this is for the sociologist more important—that a tribe is a world within itself having few external social ties, whereas a caste is by its nature a part of a larger whole being linked by multifarious ties with other castes.

The second criterion is language or dialect. The tribes speak a variety of dialects which can be shown to differ on a number of

[28] G. S. Ghurye, *The Aborigines—'so-called'—and their Future*, Gokhale Institute of Politics and Economics, 1943.

[29] V. Elwin, *The Aboriginals*, O.U.P., 1943.

important counts from the major Indian languages. This is the really crucial diacritical feature which separates 'tribal' from 'non-tribal' peasants when they come to live together in the same region, district or village. But here also there is some ambiguity. For even if we take a restricted area like Chota Nagpur we will find that there are tribes like the Oraons and Mundas which speak quite different dialects, and that there are yet others like the Bhumij who have lost their tribal dialect and now use the dominant language of the area.

In the end there is religion. Even if we regard the contrast between 'Animism' and 'Hinduism' as too crude, we might concede that there are numerous elements of religious belief and practice common to Oraons, Santals, Mundas and Hos which do not find a place in what is commonly accepted as Hinduism. But religion, unlike language, is a loose criterion, for what we encounter is a continuum without sharp breaks, and where we draw the line between 'tribal' and 'non-tribal' must remain arbitrary. N. K. Bose, who combined the perspectives of ethnography and Indology in his study of tribe and caste, was inclined to stress the continuity between the two. What he says about shifting cultivators like Juangs and Savaras deserves our attention for it applies *a fortiori* to settled agriculturists like Mundas, Oraons and Santals. 'Now, in this context the question arises as to whether groups such as the Juangs and Savaras should or should not be regarded as a part of Hindu society, or, in other words, of the social organization based on caste. Popular opinion in the state of Pal Lahara would say that even though the Juangs speak a non-Aryan language and eat the flesh of cows, pigs, snakes and other unclean animals, they ought to be counted among the Hindu communities. For after all, even among the Hindus, those who travel overseas eat unclean meat. Also the language of all Hindus is not the same. Nor is it true that they all believe in the same deity. In other words, even among those who are properly counted as a part of Hindu society, local customs and folk customs vary so much that there is no reason not to regard the Juangs as a non-Aryan community belonging to the Hindu fold.'[30]

In speaking about the Chota Nagpur tribes Bose emphasized two facts: (i) the many similarities in custom between 'tribes' and 'castes' and (ii) the many ties of interdependence between them. Bose's argument appears more persuasive in the Bengali language where the same word, *jati*, is freely used to refer to both caste and tribe.

[30] Bose, *Hindu Samajer Garhan*, op. cit., p. 14.

Bailey has taken all these points into account and has made what is probably the only serious attempt in recent times to discriminate between tribe and caste in structural terms. He warns us against the attempt 'to see particular societies disjunctively as *either* tribes *or* castes',[31] and suggests that we view them in terms of a continuum. Further, he seeks to make the distinction not in terms of the totality of behaviour but, in a more limited way, in relation to the politico-economic system, which corresponds closely to the context of this discussion. Briefly, Bailey's argument is that a caste society is 'organic' and hierarchical while a tribal society is 'segmentary' and egalitarian. He points to the fact that in the Kondmals, which he takes as an example, the relation to the land was very different among the Konds as compared to the Oriyas. About the Konds he says: 'Membership of the clan is, under the system, a condition of holding and exploiting land in the clan territory. A right to land is not achieved by subordination to anyone else, but by equality as a kinsman.'[32] In the Oriya case the right to the use of land is achieved by subordination to the members of the dominant caste. If this is the case then Kond and Oriya peasants are of two different kinds.

But we must remember that the Konds have been shifting culti-vators in the very recent past and that even at the time of Bailey's fieldwork they combined axe cultivation with plough cultivation. In considering the larger Chota Nagpur tribes like the Santals, Oraons, Mundas and Hos who have lived as settled agriculturists for a long time, we will find that the territorial identity of the clan, the corporate character of the lineage and the equality among kinsmen have ceased to be effective for a long time. If we go back to Bose's account of the Mundas referred to earlier, we will find that structurally they were ceasing to be a tribe already in the eighteenth century. Bailey himself clearly sees the limited practical value of his scheme in contemporary India where both caste and tribe are becoming rapidly transformed. He tells us at the end of his analysis that 'both caste and tribe are being merged into a different system which is neither one nor the other'.[33] This is an agrarian system whose base consists of a heterogeneous body of peasants cut up into various ethno-linguistic categories.

---

[31] Bailey, ' "Tribe" and "Caste" in India', op. cit., p. 15.
[32] Ibid., pp. 11–12.   [33] Ibid., p. 18.

5

Peasants and Workers

APART FROM academic anthropology, the tradition of Marxian inquiry has contributed much to our understanding of the peasantry. Whereas anthropologists began by viewing peasants in opposition to tribesmen, for Marxists the fundamental problem has been, and continues to be, the position of peasants in relation to workers. These two different points of departure are rooted in divergent conceptions of the relation between thought and action, and they have led to different perspectives on the peasant question. Taken together they tell us much about the nature of agrarian social structure.

There are certain striking similarities between the two approaches to the problem. Both have what may be very broadly described as an evolutionary orientation. The anthropologist not only views tribe and peasantry as two different modes of organization but sees the transformation of the one into the other as a general if not universal process. Similarly, for the Marxist, where peasants and workers co-exist in the same society, they represent two different types of socio-economic formation, one more advanced than the other.

The academic anthropologist tends to view the transformation of tribe into peasantry as a kind of natural process of development. The Marxist, on the other hand, views the transformation of peasants into workers as both a natural process and an object of political action.

The question of when and how tribesmen become peasants has been in the main an academic one. But the transformation of peasants into workers and the role of peasants and workers in the general transformation of society have been as much political as academic questions. Whether one views the social situation and economic interests of peasants and of workers as being fundamentally the same or fundamentally different depends in some measure on one's political orientations. For this reason it is not always easy to achieve clarity about the conditions of these two strata in society and their mutual relations.

The so-called dynamic conception of society is often used as a double-edged weapon. It may be used to argue that the position of peasants and of workers is the same or that it is not the same. If one chooses one can show that the interests of the two are in conflict at any given point of time. But this can be reconciled with the view that over a period of time their interests will become convergent. The absence of a universally acceptable theory of social change makes it difficult for those who are not partisans to determine the actual alignment of groups and their interests in a particular society.

It is well known that on the whole Marx himself adopted a dismissive attitude in regard to the peasantry. This has to be understood in the light of his general theory of social change and his specific interest in the transformation of capitalism into socialism. In Marx's scheme of analysis this transformation was to be spearheaded by the industrial working class. The peasantry represented not the vanguard of the new social order but the residue of the old. The centre of the political arena was to be taken up by the conflict between capitalists and workers; the peasants would at best occupy the sidelines.

Lenin's attitude towards the peasantry was manifestly different. He wrote much more about them and clearly saw them playing a more significant role in social transformation than did Marx. We must remember that Marx was writing primarily about countries like France, Germany and England. Lenin, on the other hand, always had Russia at the centre of his mind, and Russia was a backward country with a massive population of peasants. As one who was involved directly in the organization of a major political programme in a predominantly agrarian society, Lenin could not afford to adopt a dismissive attitude towards the peasantry.

In his writings on the peasantry Lenin sought to make consistent use of the Marxian tools of analysis. For although he conceded that many differences prevailed between peasants and workers, he argued that they were both coming increasingly under the influence of the capitalist economic system. This in his view was leading to a steady convergence between the vast majority of peasants and the industrial workers in the economic and political fields. As is well known, he drew much on Kautsky's study of conditions in Germany in elaborating his own arguments, although there were certain basic differences between the two points of view.

Although Lenin attached much greater significance to the peasantry than did Marx, he too believed that it was the industrial worker who would constitute the vanguard of the new social order. The peasants were to play their historic role by aligning themselves with the working class movement since the interests of the two were convergent; the task of social analysis was to demonstrate by a careful collection of data that this convergence was in fact bringing the two closer together. It is only with Mao Tse-tung and the success of the Chinese Communist movement that the peasants are brought to the centre of the historical arena. However much one might argue about the continuity of thought between Marx and Mao, no two thinkers could differ more profoundly on their assessment of the social and historical significance of the peasantry.

The success of peasant movements in China and elsewhere in the Third World has created a new image of the peasantry. A hundred years ago peasants were considered to be quintessentially backward and conservative. Today they have come to be regarded by some as having great potential for revolutionary change. Unfortunately, the revolutionary potential of the peasantry (or of any social stratum) in a country comes to be widely appreciated only after some dramatic change has taken place in its fortunes. But the task of the sociologist is not so much to speculate on what might happen or on what might have happened, as to discuss objectively the prevailing alignment of groups and categories in a society.

In discussing peasants and workers we are dealing with the system of stratification of a society or with its class structure. Some scholars would distinguish between stratification and class by saying that the former refers to the gradation of groups in a society while the latter refers to the conflict of interests between them.[1] Even though it may be possible to distinguish between the two analytically, there is in reality a great deal of convergence between them. We shall discuss

[1] Georges Gurvitch and Ralf Dahrendorf are two among many European sociologists who have argued in this way. For a brief discussion of their point of view, see my 'Ideas and Interests' in *Studies in Agrarian Social Structure*, O.U.P., 1973.

not only the place of the peasantry in the scheme of social gradation but also the conflict or identity of interests between them and other social categories.

From the sociological point of view the great merit of Lenin's work was that he did not take the peasants to be a homogeneous or undifferentiated category, but devoted himself to a serious examination of their internal structure.[2] His was very different from the view that peasants were 'like potatoes in a sack of potatoes'[3] or that they were a community of equals bound by organic ties to each other and to the land. Marx too contrasts two types of peasants, the revolutionary and enlightened peasant who looks to the future, and the conservative and superstitious peasant who looks to the past; but this contrast serves more the purpose of polemic than of scientific analysis.

As Ossowski[4] has pointed out, Lenin's subdivision of the Russian peasantry into *kulak* (or rich peasant), *stredniak* (or middle peasant) and *bedniak* (or poor peasant) has provided students of the peasantry with a conceptual scheme which is of general significance. While his ultimate aim might have been to predict and direct the political orientations of the different subdivisions in terms of a pre-existing theory of ideology, he took great pains to analyse the social and economic characteristics of each one of them.

Lenin's views on the Russian peasantry were developed in opposition to those of the *narodniki*.[5] The latter were champions of the traditional Russian *mir* which in their view was a natural, organic community of equals. They sought to resist the onslaught of external forces which might threaten the unity and harmony of the *mir*. Lenin argued that their view of the Russian *mir* was idyllic and that it bore little correspondence with existing realities. It was in this context that he relentlessly exposed the inequalities and contradictions within the peasantry itself. In his view an ideology which glorified the peasantry as a whole must inevitably justify the exploitation of the poor peasant by the rich.

[2] See V. I. Lenin, *Selected Works*, Vol. XII, International Publishers, 1943, and in it particularly 'The Agrarian Question and the "Critics of Marx" '; also his *To The Rural Poor*, Progress Publishers, 1967.

[3] This is a paraphrase of Marx's well-known statement in his *The Eighteenth Brumaire of Louis Bonaparte*, Foreign Languages Publishing House, n.d.

[4] Stanislav Ossowski, *Class Structure in the Social Consciousness*, Routledge and Kegan Paul, 1963, p. 44 n.

[5] See Lenin, *Selected Works*, op. cit.

Lenin's analyses of the Russian peasantry should make us cautious about accepting a blanket characterization of peasants being subjected to 'domination by outsiders'. For it is clear that whatever the position might have been in the past, the rich peasants about whom Lenin spoke did not necessarily occupy an underdog position, and the poor peasants were not subjected to domination only by outsiders. It is possible that Lenin exaggerated the cleavage between the rich peasants and the rural poor for reasons of polemic, but the cleavage itself could not have been his invention.

If we turn to rural society in India we will find not only inequalities between groups but also conflicts of interest between them. These inequalities and conflicts are centred in an important way around the ownership, control and use of land. In very general terms the agricultural population of India may be divided into three categories. These are (i) non-cultivating owners and tenure holders; (ii) owner-cultivators and cultivating tenants with recognized rights of tenancy; and (iii) share-croppers and agricultural labourers. In the strict sense of the term only those belonging to category (ii) are peasants; members of categories (ii) and (iii) together may be called peasants in a loose way; those belonging to category (i) cannot be described as peasants in any sense of the term.

Indian sociologists have grown accustomed to viewing the social hierarchy in terms of caste where the categories are mutually exclusive and are divided by boundaries which are sharp and clearly defined. They are inclined to be a little baffled when confronted with categories which are indefinite, ill-defined and frequently overlapping. If one has a neat and tidy mind one will find it enormously more satisfying to talk about Rajputs, Jats and Chamars than about landlords, peasants and agricultural labourers.

The difficulties in demarcating clearly the categories with which we are concerned should be emphasized. The threefold division of the peasantry by Lenin into *kulak*, *stredniak* and *bedniak* probably represented cleavages generally recognized by the people themselves so that even if the divisions cannot be precisely delimited, there is a good sociological reason for starting one's analyses with them. But what is misleading is to assume that divisions of exactly the same kind provide significant cleavages in every type of agrarian society. In the Indian case we may need a twofold or a fourfold division, or a threefold division of a somewhat different kind. The spirit of Marxian inquiry does not require that students of rural society in

India should imitate in every detail the scheme adopted by Lenin for the study of rural society in Russia.

From what has been said earlier it should be evident that the category 'peasant' is not always found in its pure form in India. It merges with the non-working landowner at one end and the landless agricultural worker at the other. This kind of overlap may be observed not only in the 'peasant' community and the 'peasant' caste but also in the peasant household if we examine it over a period of time. It is caused partly by the very sensitive inverse relation between manual work and high social status, and partly by the extreme fragmentation of landholdings.

A peasant household, in the strict sense of the term, is a household in which both men and women perform the bulk of the agricultural work on land which they themselves either own or effectively control. In India, particularly in areas of wet paddy cultivation, there has been a marked tendency for first women and then men to withdraw from agricultural work as soon as economic circumstances make it possible. When this withdrawal is complete and the land is worked by either sharecroppers or agricultural labourers, the household is no longer a peasant household but one of landowners. But the withdrawal rarely takes place in one decisive step so that there are all kinds of intermediate stages between a purely peasant household and a household of non-working landowners.

At the other end of the scale, the extreme fragmentation of holdings makes the peasant depend less and less on his own land, and more and more on work as either wage labourer or sharecropper on land owned and controlled by others. Here also there is rarely a sharp break which makes the household become solely dependent on wage labour, and there are all kinds of transitional stages between the poor peasant and the pure agricultural worker.

A word of caution needs to be introduced at this stage. The processes of increasing withdrawal from manual work and increasing dependence on wage employment appear as processes of change from the viewpoint of the individual actors involved. But they may or may not represent a change in the social system taken as a whole. There is every reason to believe that a certain amount of circulation of individuals between the kinds of roles we are considering was a normal feature of the traditional system. While this circulation has undoubtedly increased in recent times, we do not have any exact measure of either the extent or the significance of this increase.

Thus, those whom we may properly designate as peasants in India are not a clearly-defined type, but a category whose edges become easily blurred. This category, which appears as a unity in opposition to landowners, is itself internally differentiated. What is the best way of representing this internal differentiation? Before we decide to employ such blanket phrases as 'rich', 'middle' and 'poor' it may be worthwhile to enquire what they signify in terms of the structure of social relations.

Clearly, the meanings that we attach to phrases like 'rich', 'middle' and 'poor' will vary not only from one region to another but also from one point of time to another. One obvious way of differentiating between peasants is by the size of their holdings; this provides a way of classifying them according to information that is relatively easy to obtain. But there are obvious limitations in this. The productivity of land varies greatly not only from one region to another but between holdings within the same village. Further, differences in tenurial status must be taken into account; operational holdings of the same size might vary greatly in their proportions of land owned to land leased in.

In addition to the size of holding one might take into account other assets such as livestock and farm machinery. Lenin believed that the amount of livestock, particularly horses, owned gave an accurate indication of the economic position of a peasant household.[6] It would be difficult to say how far this is true in India in regard to plough cattle, for it is not uncommon for even poor peasants to own plough cattle along with which they hire themselves out for wages on land owned by wealthier people. The use of farm machinery is as yet uncommon for the country as a whole, and machinery is probably most widely used by those who are more properly described as farmers rather than peasants.

Variations in the size, status and quality of holdings, and in the nature and amount of other agricultural assets govern variations of household income among the peasantry. Even if we ignore for the time being the difficulties inherent in computing agricultural income, a subdivision of the peasantry (or of any social stratum) in terms of income will remain in some sense arbitrary. For where there is a continuous distribution of income within a certain range, there are

[6] Ibid.

no natural cutting-off points by which we can decide whether there should be two, three or four subdivisions and what these should be.[7]

An equally good if not a better way of classifying peasants is in terms of their degree of participation in the actual work of agriculture. I said that a peasant household, ideally conceived, is one whose members themselves cultivate their land and neither hire in workers from outside nor hire themselves out to work for others. But this ideal is rarely if ever fully met. Peasant households hire workers in for specific activities and peasants hire themselves out seasonally without necessarily losing the basic characteristics by which they are defined. Indeed it is not uncommon for the same household both to hire in and to hire out workers in return for wages.

Thus, using the criterion of hired work, it may be possible to classify peasants into three broad categories. Firstly, there are those who regularly depend on hired hands to supplement the labour contributed by members of the household. Secondly, there are those who regularly work for others in addition to cultivating the land which they themselves own or control. Lastly, there are those who do not hire others to work for them or hire themselves out to work for others, as well as those who do a little of both. As in the case of divisions by size of holding or income, although to a lesser extent, the cutting-off points here also may have to be arbitrarily chosen.

There will no doubt be a broad correspondence between the classification of peasants according to their size of holding (or income) and their classification according to the degree and extent of participation in work. But it will be misleading to treat the two classifications as interchangeable on the assumption that whether people engage hired workers and whether they hire themselves out for work depend solely on their economic condition. In fact the extent to which the two classifications—by size of holding and by participation in work— correspond itself differs appreciably from one culture to another.

In India peasant households which are of high social status (or believe themselves to be of high social status) generally discourage their women from working in the fields and may therefore be obliged to hire workers regularly for particular agricultural operations even

[7] For a general discussion of this problem, see Stanislav Ossowski, 'Old Notions and New Problems: Interpretations of Social Structure in Modern Society' in André Béteille (ed.), *Social Inequality*, Penguin, 1969; for a discussion relating to the agrarian social structure in an Indian state, see my 'Class Structure in an Agrarian Society' in *Studies in Agrarian Social Structure*, op. cit.

when their holdings are of small size. On the other hand, in households where there is a tradition for both men and women to do agricultural work, there may be less dependence on hired workers even when the holdings are fairly large. There is a close relationship in India between the presence of a large body of agricultural workers and the elaborate social gradation of the different types of agricultural work, and this gradation itself is not governed solely by material considerations.

In characterizing the peasantry I have emphasized all along the fact of their direct participation in manual work. Not all peasants participate in work to the same extent. There are important differences in the type of work they do according to age and sex. Some peasants hire workers more or less regularly to supplement the work done by members of the household. But participation in manual work in one form or another is a universal feature of all peasant households. From this point of view the peasantry are fundamentally different from the gentry, and there is a basic similarity between peasants and workers.

Do peasants and workers constitute a single class? Lenin raised this question and answered it categorically in the negative.[8] Peasants and industrial workers may be contrasted in a variety of ways. There are differences in their economic condition, their cultural life and their political orientation. As is well known, Marx was not prepared to regard the French peasantry of the mid-nineteenth century as a class since they lacked political consciousness and organization.[9] Do peasants become a class by the mere creation of a political association which claims to represent their interests? How does one assess the level of political consciousness among the peasantry?

Both Marx and Lenin used industrial workers as a yardstick for assessing 'class-formation' among the peasantry, and we certainly deepen our insight into the latter by viewing them alongside the former. One important difference between the two is that industrial workers are a much more clearly delimited category than peasants. The pure industrial worker is much more easy to identify than the pure peasant, particularly in a country like India with its complex tenurial history, its extreme fragmentation of holdings and its elaborate gradation of the different types of traditional manual work.

The characteristics of the Indian peasantry as a stratum (or a class)

[8] V. I. Lenin, 'The Peasantry and the Working Class' in *Selected Works*, Vol. XII, op. cit.

[9] Marx, *The Eighteenth Brumaire*, op. cit.

and their position vis-à-vis the workers may be considered in terms of various criteria. Let us consider them in terms of the following: (i) market situation; (ii) work situation; (iii) status situation; and (iv) political situation. At this stage of our enquiry only a brief indication can be given of the kinds of questions that require to be answered.

The market situation is, in David Lockwood's terms, 'the economic position narrowly conceived, consisting of source and size of income, degree of job-security, and opportunity for upward mobility'.[10] Clearly the market situations of peasants and of industrial workers are very different. The peasant is an own-account worker who controls his means of production while the industrial worker is an employee, working with instruments owned and controlled by others. Even when the peasant's income becomes increasingly responsive to market forces, it is never responsive to them in the same way as the worker's income. Further, the upward mobility of peasants (from 'poor' to 'middle' or from 'middle' to 'rich') is governed by forces which are very different from those which govern upward mobility among industrial workers; the same is of course true of downward mobility.

A point that has been recognized by authorities from Marx to Lenin is that it is in regard to economic security that peasants differ most characteristically from industrial workers. It is not as if the economic security of peasants (and particularly of small-holding peasants) is never threatened by market forces. But the impact of these forces and the time-scale over which they operate are different in the two cases, so that peasants and workers have often diametrically opposed views of what constitutes a threat to their economic security.

The work situation refers to 'the set of social relationships in which the individual is involved at work by virtue of his position in the division of labour'.[11] Marx has described the work situation of the French peasantry in characteristic terms.[12] Put in a nutshell, his argument is that the work situation of the peasant isolates him from other peasants whereas the work situation of the industrial worker brings him increasingly closer to other industrial workers.

To the extent that the family farm is the basic unit of economic organization among the peasantry, the domestic group provides the basic framework for most of the effective relations involving work;

[10] David Lockwood, *The Blackcoated Worker*, Allen and Unwin, 1958, p. 15.
[11] Ibid., p. 15.
[12] Marx, *The Eighteenth Brumaire*, op. cit.

the division of labour is governed primarily by the age and sex composition of the household. Relations involving work which extend beyond the domestic group are in the case of peasants generally confined within the local community. In the case of industrial workers, the work situation involves relations which are detached not only from the domestic context, but also to a large extent from the context of the local community.

The status situation of a class or a stratum refers to the prestige enjoyed by its members. There are major difficulties in comparing peasants with industrial workers from this point of view. For while there is an elaborate gradation of work in Indian society, there is no obvious way in which traditional types of work can be compared with those of more recent origin.

Even if one were to have a single prestige rating of the various activities in agriculture and in industry, one would still have problems of comparability. For in assessing the status situation of a stratum we have to consider not only the work performed by its members but also the degree of independence enjoyed by them in their work. Industrial activities might be rated higher than agricultural, but being an own-account worker rather than an employee might more than offset the negative value placed on agricultural work.

The political situation of a stratum or a class is to be viewed in the light of the level of political consciousness among its members and the existence of movements and associations to give expression to this consciousness in the political arena. In terms of Marx's famous dictum, a stratum does not become a class so long as there is 'merely a local interconnexion' among its members and 'the identity of their interests begets no community, no national bond and no political organization among them'.[13]

I have considered the political situation as a factor in its own right because although it clearly is affected by the market situation, the work situation and the status situation, it affects all these factors in its turn. Thus, it is well known that where there is an effective political organization among workers, they may alter their market situation as well as their work situation to their advantage.

Thus, it is not enough to say that peasants—like industrial workers —occupy an underdog position and are subjected to exploitation. Not only the manner of their exploitation but also their response to it may be different. Further, the possibilities of organizing peasant

[13] Ibid., p. 124.

movements and associations have altered vastly since Marx wrote about the French peasantry more than a hundred years ago, and there is no reason to believe as Lenin seems to have believed that such movements or associations must necessarily depend for their leadership on the organized industrial working class. How peasants will respond to their political situation cannot be determined in terms of some pre-existing general theory but will have to be established empirically for each type of society.

So far we have viewed peasants in relation to industrial workers. These are strata or classes which may be compared and contrasted but which do not interact with each other directly. In my view it is more fruitful to see peasants in relation to agricultural workers, for here we may consider not only similarities and differences but also direct interaction between the two.

There is a question of terminology which needs to be settled first of all. As Daniel Thorner has pointed out, the term 'peasant' may be used in a broad as well as a narrow sense.[14] In the narrow sense 'peasants' are smallholders who live by cultivating land which they themselves own or control. But in the broad sense, which is very commonly adopted, 'peasants' are all those who live by working on the land including sharecroppers and agricultural workers. The Marxists have more or less consistently used the word in its more narrow and rigorous meaning, and I propose to follow their usage because it is only in this way that we can explore more deeply the relationship between those who work on land they themselves control and those who work on land controlled by others.

While accepting the more rigorous definition of peasantry and the distinction implicit in it between peasants and agricultural workers, we must keep in mind the reason why the broader conception is so commonly used. For although it is both possible and desirable to make the distinction analytically, in the real world there is frequent and considerable overlap between the two categories. This has significant implications for the relations between peasants and agricultural workers. Where there is much overlap between the two categories, the relations between peasants and agricultural workers are of one kind; where the overlap is reduced and the categories become

[14] Daniel Thorner, 'Peasantry' in David L. Sils (ed.), *International Encyclopedia of the Social Sciences*, The MacMillan Company and The Free Press, 1968, pp. 503–11.

mutually exclusive, the relations are of a different kind.

India has a large population of agricultural workers. This population has grown both absolutely and relatively to the other agrarian strata over the last century, and probably with increasing rapidity over the last decade. But it has been established beyond reasonable doubt that there was a considerable population of agricultural workers at the beginning of the nineteenth century,[15] so that those who worked on the land were not a homogeneous category even at the inception of British rule.

The term 'agricultural worker' can no doubt be used narrowly to refer only to those who work for wages in cash and are bound to their employers by the cash nexus. Agricultural workers in this sense are probably of relatively recent origin, but it would be unduly restrictive to use the term in this way and to exclude workers who are paid in kind or are bound to their masters by traditional obligations. For there is much historical as well as sociological continuity between agricultural workers who are paid in cash and those who are paid in kind.

Almost exactly 30 per cent of the total workers and a little under 40 per cent of the workers in agriculture were recorded as being agricultural labourers at the 1971 census. These aggregate figures give only a very broad idea of the density and significance of agricultural labourers in the total work force. In two states, Andhra Pradesh and Kerala, agricultural labourers outnumbered cultivators or constituted more than half the total work force in agriculture, and in two others, Tamil Nadu and Bihar, there were nearly as many agricultural labourers as cultivators.

The figures given in the provisional tables of the 1971 census will have to be treated with some caution for they show some puzzling features which are not very easy to account for. Between 1961 and 1971 the proportion of agricultural labourers among all workers is shown to have increased from 18.87 to 29.98 per cent. In several states such as the Punjab, Haryana and Rajasthan these proportions have more than doubled. Census figures sometimes show dramatic changes which on closer examination prove to be illusory.[16] But what-

---

[15] Dharma Kumar, *Land and Caste in South India*, Cambridge University Press, 1965.

[16] See J. Krishnamurty, 'Working Force in 1971 Census: Some Exercises on Provisional Results', *Economic and Political Weekly*, Vol. VII, No. 3, January 1972, pp. 115–18.

ever the case may be, it seems certain that there is not only a large population of agricultural workers in the country but also that it is on the increase.

Some of the problems we faced in comparing peasants with industrial workers are easily resolved when we compare them with agricultural workers. The market situation of agricultural workers is almost invariably inferior to that of peasants, probably even in those limited areas where wages have shown a substantial rise due either to increased production as in the Punjab or to organized political action as in Kerala. The transformation of the peasant into an agricultural worker is still the most general indicator of the deterioration of the market situation of the former.

The work situation of agricultural workers may or may not be similar to that of peasants. Where they are employed in their own village on a more or less permanent basis and where members of the household are employed together, their work situation may not differ very much from that of owner-cultivators. But agricultural workers are having increasingly to work on somewhat different terms. Wage employment in agriculture is becoming more contractual, and when this happens, the different members of the household may not be employed together or even in the same village. Even here it might be misleading to characterize agricultural workers as a 'rural proletariat' because important differences continue to exist between their work situation and that of industrial workers.

The status of agricultural workers is unambiguously inferior to that of peasants. While they both do the same general kind of work, those who are employed for wages—whether in cash or in kind—are usually burdened with the more onerous and arduous tasks. It is well known that members of the higher 'peasant' castes, such as Jats, who have lost their land may be prepared to work as tenants but are reluctant to hire themselves out as wage labourers, primarily for reasons of status; and what applies to men applies even more strongly to women.

The political situation of agricultural workers reveals a certain ambiguity. Their 'underdog position' makes it in one sense easy to organize them for programmes of radical change. But their sense of economic insecurity and social inferiority also makes their organization in another sense peculiarly vulnerable. As in all such cases, the strength or weakness of their organization depends on the character of the class against which it is directed.

The political union of agricultural workers has been successful in certain limited parts of the country. On the whole it has been more successful in the areas of wet paddy cultivation, particularly in some districts of South India such as Alleppey in Kerala and Tanjore in Tamil Nadu. In these districts the most successful agrarian organizations are in fact the Agricultural Workers' Unions rather than the Kisan Sabhas which represent the interests of the peasants in general.

It has been argued by some that agricultural wages show a substantial increase only when agricultural workers have a sufficiently strong political organization to demand successfully this increase. Pranab Bardhan has sought to confirm this argument by a comparative study of agricultural wages in the different parts of the country. According to Bardhan, in Ludhiana district (Punjab), where production increased substantially between 1962-3 and 1967-8, the rise in real wages was small whereas in Allepey and Palghat districts in Kerala they rose much more in the same period.[17]

T. K. Oommen has examined in detail the factors associated with the rise in the real wages of agricultural workers in Alleppey district.[18] This rise has been attended by widespread and intense agrarian conflict. Among the economic factors responsible for the conflict are a large concentration of landless labourers and the extreme fragmentation of holdings. Even at the 1961 census over half the total workers in agriculture were agricultural labourers, and a more recent survey shows that nearly 90 per cent of the operational holdings are of 2.5 acres or less.[19] Although there is much landlessness and fragmentation of holdings throughout India, these figures must be considered unusually high.

There are two specific features of the economic situation of agricultural workers in Alleppey district which deserve attention. The first is the considerable measure of geographical mobility among them. Oommen tells us, 'Roads and transport and communications are well developed in Alleppey district, and this immensely facilitates the movement of men. It is a common sight during harvest seasons that men and women commute in buses to agricultural fields.'[20] Secondly,

[17] Pranab Bardhan, 'Green Revolution and Agricultural Labourers', *Economic and Political Weekly*, Vol. V, Nos. 29–31, July 1970, pp. 1239–46.

[18] T. K. Oommen, 'Agrarian Tension in a Kerala District: An Analysis', *Indian Journal of Industrial Relations*, Vol. 7, No. 2, 1971, pp. 229–68.

[19] Cited in Oommen, op. cit.

[20] Oommen, op. cit., p. 241.

the same person is quite frequently an agricultural as well as an industrial worker. Both these features are related to the distinctive ecology of settlements in Kerala where rural-urban differences are in general much weaker than elsewhere in the country.

According to Oommen, 'The first agricultural labour union in Kuttanad was formed in 1939, as a branch of the Travancore Karshaka Thozhilali (agricultural labour) Union (TKTU).'[21] From its inception the TKTU was controlled largely by the Communist Party and, with the split in it in 1964, there was a corresponding split in the TKTU into the Kerala Karshaka Thozhilali Federation controlled by the CPI and the Kerala State Karshaka Thozhilali Union controlled by the CPI(M), the latter emerging as the more powerful organization.

The Kerala Government set up a 'tripartite committee consisting of the representatives of the government, farmers, and agricultural labourers'[22] in July 1957. Since then the representatives of the agricultural labourers have extracted a number of concessions in wages and conditions of work, although their effectiveness here as elsewhere has been weakened considerably by inter-union rivalries. Oommen's analysis shows that the relative success of agricultural workers in Alleppey cannot be explained by any one factor, but owes itself to a combination of various factors which may be individually present elsewhere but usually not in the same combination.

Elsewhere we have discussed in some detail the factors that have contributed to the increasing political strength of agricultural workers in Tanjore district in Tamil Nadu.[23] There also there is a powerful Agricultural Workers' Union controlled by the CPM which has played an important part in bargaining for higher wages at tripartite meetings between representatives of employers, employees and Government. I too have argued, like Oommen, that the success of the Agricultural Workers' Union in Tanjore owes itself to a combination of various factors although these are not exactly the same as those identified by Oommen in his analysis of Alleppey district.

The materials from Alleppey as well as Tanjore bring out one point on which comment is required. In discussing relations between employers and employees in agriculture one talks in a loose way of landlords and landless labourers. The point that I would like to make is that very probably a substantial number of the employers of

[21] Ibid., p. 246. [22] Ibid., p. 251.
[23] 'Agrarian Relations in Tanjore District, South India' in my *Studies in Agrarian Social Structure*, op. cit.

agricultural labourers in both Alleppey and Tanjore would be better described as peasants than as landlords. For these are areas in which over half the people working in agriculture are agricultural labourers and in which the vast majority of operational holdings—in Alleppey district over 98 per cent—are of less than 5 acres. Clearly, many landless labourers must be employed by people who themselves have dwarf holdings. Granted that pure, self-employed peasants must be somewhat uncommon and that we have to deal rather with those who more or less approximate to the pure type, there must be serious conflicts of interest between 'peasants' and agricultural workers.

The presence of these conflicts and the problems created by them for leaders of peasant movements and associations are clearly revealed when we turn to a different area, i.e. West Bengal. West Bengal has a long tradition of agrarian movements and, along with Kerala, it has had the most powerful Kisan Sabha among all the states in India. But the agricultural workers have failed to unite effectively and they have not been able to raise wages and improve conditions of work through organized political action as in Kerala or in Tanjore district.

There are certain differences in objective condition between West Bengal on the one hand and Kerala and Tanjore district on the other. West Bengal does not have as large a concentration of agricultural workers as either of the two other areas. But more important than that, the pure agricultural labourer who lives only by working for wages is far less common in West Bengal than in Kerala or in Tanjore district. There is a fairly high degree of overlap between cultivating-owners, sharecroppers and wage labourers in most districts of West Bengal. As a consequence, the employer-employee relationship in agriculture has not assumed the importance in this state that it has in some of the areas in the South.

In West Bengal 'cultivators' and 'agricultural labourers' are not only mixed categories economically, but they are also socially very heterogeneous. Agricultural workers are divided into caste Hindus, Harijans and Adivasis. The distinction between Harijans and Adivasis is quite marked in West Bengal, and is often reflected in the settlement pattern of the village. In Tanjore district those talukas which show a preponderance of agricultural workers also show a preponderance of Harijans within this category. By contrast, the many distinctions of status among agricultural workers in West Bengal act as an obstacle to their effective political organization.

The first major agrarian struggle organized by the Kisan Sabha in Bengal was the Tebhaga movement of 1946-7. This movement sought an increase in the share of the sharecropper from one-half to two-thirds, and other improvements in his economic situation. It was organized by the then united Kisan Sabha of the then undivided Bengal. Sunil Sen, the historian of the Tebhaga movement who himself took a leading part in it, gives us some indication of the dilemmas faced by the Kisan Sabha in Bengal from almost its very inception. 'It seems that the overriding consideration of the Kisan Sabha was to preserve peasant unity, and the emphasis was on those demands which corresponded to the immediate interests of all categories of peasants, so that a broad peasant movement could be built up as part of the developing anti-imperialist movement.'[24] In his own account of the Tebhaga movement, Sen systematically ignores the distinction made since Lenin between 'peasants' and 'agricultural workers', and talks frequently of rich peasants, middle peasants, poor peasants and landless peasants (comprising sharecroppers and agricultural workers). Now it is a moot question as to how far the interests of these categories did in fact converge at the time of the Tebhaga movement in 1946–7.

The Tebhaga movement failed by and large to achieve its objectives. But the demands which it had raised continued to exist. There was massive agrarian unrest in West Bengal again between 1968 and 1970. One important difference between the two movements is that the more recent one was organized while United Front governments dominated by the CPI(M) were in office. It was also on a somewhat larger scale and had a more ambitious programme of demands. But the central issue once again was the general one of land to the tiller and the specific one of better terms for the sharecropper. Further, once again the programme sought to emphasize peasant unity and to assume an identity of interests between poor peasants, sharecroppers and agricultural workers.

It is difficult to say what permanent gains were achieved by the Kisan Sabha on behalf of the poor peasants and sharecroppers. But agricultural workers did not gain very much, and agricultural wages in West Bengal remain fairly low as compared to Kerala and many other parts of the country.

Some of the structural reasons which impeded the development of

[24] Sunil Sen, *Agrarian Struggle in Bengal: 1946–47*, People's Publishing House, 1972, p. 80.

an effective union of agricultural workers in West Bengal have earlier been explained. If one reads the documents of the Bengal (and later West Bengal) Kisan Sabha over the last thirty years, one will be struck by the ambivalent attitude of its leadership towards such a union.[25] In the forties the problem was discussed in great detail, and the general opinion was that such a union would be desirable. One finds the same opinion being expressed in the late sixties and the same lack of action. The contrast between Kerala and West Bengal shows that the situation of agricultural workers cannot improve substantially unless they are effectively organized, and that this organization itself presupposes certain structural conditions which are not universally present.

[25] See my 'Peasant Associations and the Agrarian Class Structure' in *Studies in Agrarian Social Structure*, op. cit.

6

Marxism and Modern Sociology

IN INDIA TODAY the academic sociologist who seeks to establish a dialogue with practising Marxists must take the risk of having his fingers burnt. It seems that Marxists are quite happy to have sociologists study caste, kinship and ritual, and to make occasional jibes at the triviality of sociological research. But when the sociologist turns to such subjects as the social organization of production, the agrarian class structure or peasant movements and associations, he becomes at once the object of deep suspicion.

The uneasy relationship in which one finds Marxism and academic sociology in contemporary India is by no means unique. The tension between the two approaches, or the two perspectives is ultimately rooted in two possible ways of relating thought and action. Hence it has a kind of universal character, although it manifests itself differently in different places and times.

It is important to remember that academic sociology (including social anthropology) was introduced into India from Britain and America at a time when there was in these countries an almost complete separation between Marxism and sociology. Certainly in most British and American universities between the two Wars people were inclined to believe that sociology was one thing and Marxism quite another, and there was very little ground on which the two could meet. It has been pointed out earlier how Indian scholars inherited from Britain and America the unfortunate distinction between sociology and social anthropology. It can be argued, though only up to a point, that the prevailing separation between sociology and Marxism in India is an unfortunate by-product of the same inheritance.

European sociology has been on the whole much more responsive to Marxism, and the recent growth of interest in Marxism among Anglo-American sociologists is at least partly due to the increasingly easy availability in English translations of works written originally in French, German and Polish. In talking about Marxism no less than about sociology we must not lose sight of the specificity of national intellectual traditions. Marxism has permeated intellectual debate in the European countries to a far greater extent than in Britain or America, and European thinkers are inclined to be more than a little self-conscious about the special character of their intellectual heritage.

In India we tend to overlook the fact that there has been in Europe a close relationship—whether of affinity or of hostility—between Marxism and sociology. France provides a good example of the varieties of dialogue between the two, partly because of the distinctiveness of its own intellectual tradition and partly because it has been an intellectual home for scholars from so many European countries.

In a long chapter entitled 'The Sociology of Karl Marx', Georges Gurvitch, one of Europe's leading sociologists, wrote, 'The object of this study . . . is to show that Marx was the greatest and the least dogmatic of all the founders of sociology.'[1] Gurvitch did much to attract the attention of academic sociologists to the writings of the young Marx, and to build up through his own writings a dialectical sociology. Gurvitch's colleague at the University of Paris, Professor Raymond Aron, has also grappled with the ideas of Marx during most of his career, but in a different spirit: he has sought relentlessly to expose the dogmas of Marxism and to trace them back to their roots in the writings of Marx.[2]

Between Gurvitch's active enthusiasm for Marx and Aron's equally active critique of Marxism various positions are possible. One is that of Professor Lévi-Strauss who wrote: 'When I was about seventeen I was initiated into Marxism by a young Belgian socialist whom I met on a holiday. . . . Reading Marx was for me all the more enthralling in that I was making my first contact, by way of that great thinker, with the philosophical current that runs from Kant to Hegel. A whole world was opened to me. My excitement has never cooled: and rarely do I tackle a problem in sociology or ethnology without having first

---

[1] Georges Gurvitch, *La Vocation actuelle de la Sociologie*, Presses Univérsitaires de France, 1963, Vol. II, p. 220.

[2] Raymond Aron, *The Opium of the Intellectuals*, Secker and Warburg, 1957; also his *Main Currents in Sociological Thought*, Penguin, 1968, Vol. 1.

set my mind in motion by reperusal of a page or two from the
18 Brumaire of Louis Bonaparte or the *Critique of Political Economy*.'[3]

And yet when Lévi-Strauss wrote a brilliant, profound and scholarly article on French sociology[4] he did not feel the need to mention
Marx even once or to refer to any of his basic ideas.

Why are so many people instinctively enchanted, as it were, by the
idea of Marxism? Why are so many others, in an equally unreasoning
way, repelled by it? These are not just abstract or idle questions, but
must remain with us while we seek to understand the relationship
between Marxism and sociology in India.

What kind of a relationship should one expect in India between
Marxism and sociology in the years to come? In the absence of any
effective or serious debate between the two, it is inevitable that the
problem be posed first in somewhat formal terms. It seems that the
relationship between Marxism and sociology can be formulated from
three points of view. The first is that Marxism provides the basic
framework which can retain its fundamental character while absorbing the more fruitful findings of sociology. The second is that sociology
is the basic discipline which must grow by accommodating the
empirically testable ideas of Marx and of the more creative adherents
of Marxism; this is my own point of view. There is however a third
position which denies the very possibility of a Marxist sociology and
insists that Marxism and sociology are by their nature irreconcilable.

The clearest expression of the first point of view is to be found in
the writings of contemporary Soviet sociologists. As is well known,
in the Soviet Union first 'bourgeois' sociology and then sociology
pure and simple came under a cloud during the Stalinist regime. The
subject has been revived again, and Soviet sociologists have since the
mid-fifties presented their point of view at international conferences,
and have also made their work increasingly available to the outside
world through a fair number of English translations.[5]

Soviet sociologists maintain a distinction between Marxist and
bourgeois sociology. Osipov has set forward in clear terms the relations

---

[3] Claude Lévi-Strauss, *Tristes Tropiques* (English tr.), Atheneum, 1963, p. 61.

[4] Claude Lévi-Strauss, 'French Sociology' in G. Gurvitch and W. E. Moore
(eds.), *Twentieth Century Sociology*, The Philosophical Library, 1945.

[5] For a brief survey of Soviet Sociology see Alex Simirenko, *Soviet Sociology*,
Routledge and Kegan Paul, 1967.

between historical materialism, social philosophy and sociology. 'Historical materialism as a science concerns general laws governing the emergence, development and changes of socio-economic formations.'[6] The subject matter of social philosophy is 'the study of the specificity of manifestation of dialectical materialist laws (consciousness and being, transition of quantitative to qualitative changes, etc.) in social life and the discovery of new dialectical aspects in the light of modern social development'.[7] Sociology, as one of the specific social sciences, is assigned a more limited sphere. Sociologists study 'the social structure of society (inter-class and intra-class relationships, the social institutions that regulate these relationships), the development and interaction of the systems and organizations within society.'[8]

In more concrete terms, Soviet sociologists have concentrated on the study of occupational strata and ethnic groups. They have also studied attitudes to work and ceremonial life in the broad context of the change towards a more rational and secular social order. These studies use methods of investigation and exposition that are broadly similar to those commonly used by sociologists in other parts of the world.

There are two features of Soviet sociology that call for comment. The first is the pragmatic attitude towards the distinction between Marxist and bourgeois sociology: while it is stressed in principle, it is frequently ignored in practice. The second and much more significant feature is a new way of viewing the relationship between 'base' and 'superstructure'. Soviet sociologists are increasingly arguing that there are various areas of social life that are not covered properly by either, and are best characterized as 'extra-superstructural'; these, according to Afanasyev, include such socio-economic formations as clan, tribe, national group, family and marriage, and some public organizations.[9] Whether this way of representing social reality is a deviation from Marxism or an extension of it, I leave it to the specialists to decide.

The second orientation, which gives to the ideas of Marx a position of importance *within* sociology, has governed the works of a long line of European scholars from Weber through Mannheim to Aron. While

[6] G. Osipov, *Sociology*, Progress Publishers, 1969, p. 9.
[7] Ibid., p. 9.   [8] Ibid., p. 20.
[9] V. G. Afanasyev, *The Scientific Management of Society*, Progress Publishers: 1971, pp. 26–7.

acknowledging the outstanding contribution of Marx to the under-standing of social life, these authors have viewed this contribution in a critical light, and, consequently have often been characterized, wrongly in my view, as anti-Marxist. It has been said of Weber that his work was a 'long dialogue with the ghost of Marx', and Mann-heim's work has been described as 'bourgeois Marxism'.

The task of sociology, as I see it, is to study the dialectical relation-ship between ideas and interests, or between the fundamental cultural categories of a society and the distribution of power in it.[10] It is hard to concede that any single historical person (or group of persons owing allegiance to a particular corpus of work) has a superior claim to the appropriation of this task. Among sociologists who wrote in the present century, Weber's work is perhaps the best example of these fundamental concerns. He was concerned not so much with the study of power and of culture in the abstract as with their nature and interrelations in actually existing societies. There are other sociologists whose work shows the same basic concerns, although most have in practice concentrated on one or another aspect of specific human societies.

One can certainly trace back the basic concern with the relation-ship between ideas and interests to the work of Marx and indeed it is this which provides continuity between Marx and modern sociology. However, it is fruitful to trace continuities only within a living system of ideas. Hence the contribution of Marx to the creation of the socio-logical perspective acquires meaning only if we regard his theories as not final, his concepts as not fixed and his method as amenable to modification in the light of experience.

From our point of view the first thing to remember is that Marx wrote primarily about particular societies—Germany, France, Eng-land—and a particular social transformation. Asian societies in a state of transition a hundred years after Marx's time have their own modes of existence and consciousness. How can we hope to grasp these if, like theologians, we attach ourselves obstinately to the theories, concepts and methods embedded in a given set of texts?

Finally, we come to the third position according to which Marxism and sociology are by their nature irreconcilable. Perhaps it is the view

<hr>

[10] See my 'Ideas and Interests' in André Béteille, *Studies in Agrarian Social Structure*, Oxford University Press. 1973; also André Béteille, 'The Politics of "Non-Antagonistic" Strata', *Contributions to Indian Sociology*, New Series, No. III, 1969.

held by the majority in India among both practising Marxists and academic sociologists, although I am not aware that it has been explicitly formulated by any. It would be interesting to have an Indian expression of this point of view so that we can know whether there are any fresh arguments in its support or whether the arguments are the same as those of European thinkers.

Among Europeans the view that denies the very possibility of a Marxist sociology is expressed most forcefully by Georg Lukács and his followers. Interestingly, in Europe it is the Marxists who reject the possibility of an effective dialogue between Marxism and sociology; the sociologists are more willing to have such a dialogue. In India, on the other hand, both sociologists and Marxists usually view each other with roughly the same degree of suspicion.

Lucien Goldmann, whose work is much respected among European Marxists, wrote in *Le Dieu Caché* that from the viewpoint of Marxism 'sociology is impossible for the Marxist seeks to be practical and revolutionary'.[11] Later, in an article entitled 'Y a-t-il une sociologie marxiste?',[12] he reiterated the same point and argued that a Marxist sociology was not possible. Goldmann's ideas echo those of Lukács who has been probably the most influential Marxist thinker in recent times. Both Lukács and Goldmann would reject any attempt to separate 'judgements of fact' from 'judgements of value' as a denial of revolutionary praxis. For them the core of Marxism lies in this praxis which is based on and is the expression of the fundamental unity of theory and practice. Sociology, they would argue, is by its nature anti-Marxist in so far as it seeks to separate facts from values and defines its task independently of a revolutionary praxis.

The position of Lukács may be stated in yet more concrete terms.[13] All systems of ideas have a class basis. Sociology has its basis in the class interests of the bourgeoisie and is to that extent 'historical'. Marxism is rooted in the class interests of the proletariat and is not 'historical' but 'universal', since in the modern world only the proletariat constitutes the true subject of history. At this point the Indian sociologist must surely ask who constitute the proletariat or the true subject of history in India. The equation of the organized prole-

[11] Lucien Goldmann, *Le Dieu caché*, Gallimard, 1955, p. 98.

[12] Lucien Goldmann, 'Y a-t-il une sociologie marxiste?', *Les Temps modernes* No. 140, October 1957.

[13] Georg Lukács, *Histoire et Conscience de Classe*, Les Editions de Minuit, 1960.

tariat with underprivileged humanity, which is implicit in European Marxism, is in the Indian case both false and misleading.

Why is there in India, as elsewhere, this vast seedbed of mutual hostility and suspicion between Marxists and sociologists? I do not for a moment believe that all this can be eliminated by a mere act of will. But an effective dialogue can certainly help to delimit the area of disagreement and to identify its true nature and sources. An effective dialogue will be one which relates itself to the Indian experience and particularly to the agrarian social structure in India.

Mutual hostility is often sustained by a distorted image of the object of one's hostility. It is well known that the founder of Marxism had great contempt for the founder of sociology. Marx wrote in a letter, '... as a Party man I have a thoroughly hostile attitude towards Comte's philosophy, while as a scientific man I have a very poor opinion of it.'[14] Now Comte not only invented the term 'sociology', but in Marx's time the subject as such was in Europe identified with his system of positive philosophy. Gurvitch's observation that Marx was the least dogmatic of the founders of sociology becomes clear when we remember that the other principal founder was Comte, for Comte was not only dogmatic, but in his later years an eccentric person. But contemporary sociology—or even the sociology of Durkheim and Weber—bears little resemblance to the somewhat preposterous system constructed by the man who gave their names to both positivism and sociology.

Apart from what one might regard as the accidents of history, there are other issues to consider. It is a matter of experience that the exponents of two systems of idea are often most intolerant of each other not when their ideas are totally different but when they are in most respects basically similar. There is in the realm of ideas as in that of real social relations what the anthropologist describes as 'sibling rivalry'. It is worth considering that the mutual intolerance of Marxists and sociologists owes itself to the basic similarity of their projects rather than to their basic difference.

Both Marxism and sociology concern themselves with the whole of man's experience as a member of society in this world, here and now. Economics and political science deal with specific sectors of society, and history deals with the past rather than the present. The

[14] Marx to Beesly in a letter dated 12 June 1871; see Karl Marx and Friedrich Engels, *Correspondence, 1846–1895*, National Book Agency, 1945, p. 277.

historian can seek refuge in the past, and the economist in his sphere of technical competence. It is difficult to see how the sociologist can avoid confrontation with the Marxist on his own chosen ground.

It is no accident that Marxists can find a place for sociology only by confining the subject within restricted limits. Sartre, for instance, is prepared to accept sociology as an 'auxiliary discipline', but the preference is for a sociology of a very particular kind: 'The more sociology is presented as a hyper-empiricism, the easier is its integration into Marxism.'[15] Similarly, in my experience, Indian Marxists are quite willing to tolerate sociology so long as it confines itself to problems of the 'superstructure'. It hardly needs to be said that sociologists may not feel obliged to accept these arbitrary limitations on their discipline.

Philosophers like Sartre freely castigate sociology for its shallow empiricism, its not having any 'principles', any theory. I think it is only fair to say that sociology has been since its birth in search of a general theory without having really found one. Various theories do emerge from time to time—the general theory of action, symbolic interaction theory, conflict theory—but none of these really corresponds to what would be acceptable as 'theory' in the natural sciences or even in a discipline like economics.

Marx also had a theory about the growth and decay of capitalism in West European society. This theory contained a number of predictions which clearly did not come true. I am prepared to agree with Lukács that one should not be obliged to renounce Marxism solely because some or most of the *results* of Marx's research have been made obsolete by subsequent events or subsequent research.[16] For what really matters is the method or the approach to the study of social reality developed by Marx.

Further, I do not see why one should be obliged to choose between a 'totalizing theory' and a 'shallow empiricism'. This kind of dichotomy is perhaps well suited to the style and temper of a philosopher, but it cannot satisfy those who seek seriously to understand social reality without having either the capacity or the confidence to construct their own general theory. If such a theory is not already available and if it is not within each man's capacity to construct one, then what is to be done by the ordinary person who might also have a serious interest in understanding human societies?

[15] Jean-Paul Sartre, *The Problem of Method*, Methuen and Co., 1963, p.82.
[16] Lukács, *Histoire et Conscience de Classe*, op. cit.

A sharp dichotomy between 'totalizing theory' and 'shallow empiricism' is not only unreasonable but also pernicious. In those who believe that they have such a theory it encourages an attitude of disdain towards 'mere fact finding'. Many Indian Marxists appear to believe that they already know what are the basic features of this society, what are the mechanisms by which it is being transformed from 'feudalism' to 'capitalism' and what shape it will take in the years to come; they have not found it necessary to study in detail the facts about rural society as their counterparts did in China or Russia. This is the main reason why Marxists have so little to tell us about the *real* characteristics of Indian society as distinct from the characteristics predicated by their theory.

The attitude that we must first have our theory right and then turn our attention to facts is often an attitude of evasion. It is found among both Marxists and academic sociologists. It is an attitude of evasion because either the correct theory is never found or it exists from the very start, in which case the collection of facts is not expected to make much difference.

There is of course much more than an approach to the study of society in the work of Marx, although some believe that this is the most important part of it. It goes without saying that what we are discussing here is Marx's approach to the study of society—his ideas about the structure of societies, their inherent contradictions and the changes which arise from these.

It is not easy to find agreement among the experts on what is the correct Marxist approach to the study of society. There are several texts written by Marx which cannot always be reconciled with each other, and each text can be interpreted in several ways. Perhaps the clearest text is the one in the famous 'Preface' which begins with the statement, 'In the social production of their life, men enter into definite relations that are indispensable and independent of their will . . .' and concludes with the statement: 'The bourgeois relations of production are the last antagonistic form of the social process of production. . . .'[17] This text has the advantage that Marx himself described it as representing the approach which he arrived at after long years of study and reflection.

[17] Karl Marx, 'Preface' to *A Contribution to the Critique of Political Economy*, in K. Marx and F. Engels, *Selected Works*, Foreign Languages Publishing House, 1951, Vol. I, pp. 328-9.

The text referred to contains three sets of statements. There are statements about the structure of society, including its differentiation into basic structure and superstructure. There are statements about contradictions within the base, and between the base and the super-structure; contradictions which manifest themselves in social conflict. And there are statements about change, including a specification of the stages through which societies transform themselves. These state-ments are tightly linked together in this brief and concise text which is probably more impressive than anything of its kind written by a sociologist before or after.

The very first sentence defines what I would describe as the socio-logical aims of Marx. One might have difficulties with the exact meaning of the phrase 'social production of their life'. But the state-ment that 'men enter into definite relations that are indispensable and independent of their will' is not only unambiguous, but one which must be the starting-point of every kind of sociological analysis. Academic sociologists cannot fail to note that it anticipates Durk-heim's famous statement that social facts are things and, as things, they are characterized by exteriority and constraint.[18]

The distinction between the base, i.e. the 'totality of relations of production' which constitutes the 'economic structure of society', and the superstructure is also valuable provided one considers it as an heuristic device and not a dogma. It is an error to think that socio-logists in general regard all the structures of society to be equally important. What most of them would question is whether the distinc-tion between 'basic structure' and 'superstructure' is one which can be established once and for all; for the rest, many of them assign crucial importance to the economic structure of society.

The contradictions within the base, and between the base and the superstructure are reflected in the conflict of interests among indivi-duals and groups. The idea that interests and their conflicts are socially structured seems to me the most original and fruitful contri-bution of Marx to sociology. The study of class and of class conflict is rooted in a sociology of interests of which Marx, more than any-body else, laid the foundation. Marx himself saw not only the conflict of classes but the division of labour itself as being rooted in the structure of interests.

Marx argued that ideals and values which are projected as being general or universal are often masks which cover the interests of a

[18] Emile Durkheim, *The Rules of Sociological Method*, The Free Press, 1938.

8

particular class. The mask is not always consciously worn but is for that reason no less there. In *The Eighteenth Brumaire* he showed that not only classes, but organizations such as the bureaucracy might also have 'objective' interests.

The important step in the study of interests is to go beyond the individual and to see how interests are socially structured. 'How is it that personal interests always develop, against the will of individuals, into class interests, into common interests which acquire independent existence in relation to the individual persons, and in their independence assume the form of general interests?'[19] Thus interests have a dual role; they unite people into a class and they divide one class from another although this division may be masked by an ideology.

Marx realized that although interests are socially structured, there is no simple way of identifying their structures; there is in this sense a basic difference of attitude between Marx and the Marxists. Historical materialism might reveal a certain general direction of movement, but the conflict and combination of classes must be related to actually existing interests which are specific to each society at a given stage of its development. *The Eighteenth Brumaire* is a masterly analysis of the complex interplay of interests among the different classes and strata in mid-nineteenth century France.

Indian Marxists have generally assumed a certain structure of interests to prevail in Indian society whereas Marx showed in his writings on France and Germany that such structures are in fact too complex for it to be possible to determine their nature in advance. Academic sociologists have, in their turn, generally ignored the structure of interests in their study of rural Indian society; they have concentrated on common values, and on institutions like caste, kinship and religion which express these common values in their clearest form.

I have stated elsewhere,[20] borrowing an argument from Leach,[21] that social anthropologists who have worked in the Indian field have taken their basic theoretical framework from Durkheim rather than Marx. This has led them to neglect those areas of social life in which the interplay of conflicting interests is most clearly manifest. It is in

[19] Karl Marx and Friedrich Engels, *The German Ideology*, Progress Publishers, 1968, p. 270.

[20] Béteille, 'The Politics of "Non-Antagonistic" Strata', op. cit.

[21] E. R. Leach, *The Political Systems of Highland Burma*, G. Bell and Sons, 1954, p. 7.

this context that the themes that have been developed in the earlier essays acquire their significance.

The ownership, control and use of land generate interests that combine and conflict in various ways. The interplay of these interests is easy to observe at the level of interpersonal relations—say, between landlord and tenant, or between cultivator and wage labourer—and such observations are a matter of everyday experience. But what the sociologist owes to Marx is a method, which in India has been used all too sparingly, designed to study these interests in a systematic way, to identify patterns among them and to relate them to the structure of groups and categories, and in particular to the cleavages between classes and between strata.

It should by now be evident why I paid so much attention to the question of what we should mean by a peasant society. The concept of peasant society was introduced into the field of Indian studies through the work of Redfield who was on the whole insensitive to the interplay of conflicting material interests. Those who studied rural India under this kind of inspiration concentrated on the common cultural characteristics of what they mistakenly categorized as a peasant society, ignoring or neglecting the profound cleavages that have always existed in it.

What is called the peasant community in India is often deeply divided within itself. The Indian village often contains both non-working landowners and landless agricultural workers in addition to other groups and categories. To describe such a village as a community of peasants is to limit the possibility of investigating one of the most interesting features of a social system, i.e. its internal structure of interests. To take as one's point of departure that kind of investigation is to throw open one of the most important features of real societies, their division into conflicting groups and categories.

Just as it is misleading to ignore certain differences, it can also be misleading to ignore certain similarities. By stressing religion and culture, Indian anthropologists have sought persistently to draw a line between tribe and peasantry. I have tried to show that this line is mostly an arbitrary one. Those who work on the land have similar interests whether they speak Bengali or Santali, or practise Hinduism or Animism. There may be differences in their life styles—which are by no means to be discounted—but their life chances are broadly the same.

Finally, the problem of peasants and workers has also to be exa-

8A

mined within the framework of a sociology of interests. Are the interests of peasants and of workers fundamentally the same, or are they fundamentally different? Our ideas on these questions are vague and the facts at our disposal are limited and ambiguous. I do not believe that our ideas will ever become clear unless we observe directly the ways in which 'tribesmen', 'peasants' and workers organize their interests in the actual course of their lives.

Marx's analyses of the dynamics of real societies show us that people whose interests appear to be the same are often divided, even as people whose interests appear to be different often come together. It is not easy to follow Marx in this kind of work, for it requires unusual qualities of observation and of imagination. It is much easier and less vexing to apply the 'laws' of dialectical materialism to explain or explain away what is happening or is supposed to be happening in our complex society. But Marx's work is of value to the sociologist not for any laws that he is believed to have discovered but for its profound insight—which is a perennial source of inspiration to students of human society—into the social bases of human conflict.

It was Marx more than any other thinker who made sociologists aware of the inescapable nature of conflict in human societies. And more than anybody else, it was Marx who provided sociology with a method for exposing the mystifications of idea systems which seek to demonstrate the essential harmony of interests in this or that society. Yet Marx also talked about societies free from conflict and antagonism as if he was talking about real societies of the future. And others have used his arguments to assert that some particular historically-existing society has actually progressed beyond the stage of antagonism and conflict.

The famous passage from the 'Preface', referred to earlier, concludes with the statement: 'The bourgeois relations of production are the last antagonistic form of the social process of production—antagonistic not in the sense of individual antagonism, but of one arising from the social condition of life of the individuals; at the same time the productive forces developing in the womb of bourgeois society create the material conditions for the solution of that antagonism. This social formation brings, therefore, the prehistory of human society to a close.'[22] I think it is abundantly clear that Marx meant this statement to be taken literally. I also think that this

[22] Marx and Engels, *Selected Works*, op. cit., p. 329.

kind of statement is impossible to reconcile with the sociological perspective, and, if I may add, with the most fruitful and original ideas of Marx himself. What is original in Marx is his understanding of contradiction and conflict: there is nothing original in his conception of a classless society.

The distinction between 'class societies' and 'classless societies' is an important feature of Marxian thought, and from this point of view Marxism differs greatly from modern sociology. Sociologists have studied in detail a far larger range of societies than were accessible to systematic investigation in Marx's time. These studies have shown that inequality and conflict are inherent features of all human societies, including the technologically-primitive tribal societies.

No doubt the distinction made by Marxists can be logically sustained by devising appropriate definitions. As Aron has put it, 'If you define classes with reference to private ownership of the means of production, nothing is easier to make the former vanish by hoping to suppress the latter.'[23] Since Stalin's time in the Soviet Union and in East European countries scholars have talked about the replacement of 'classes' by 'strata' in their society. The relations between classes are in their view antagonistic, being based on property, while the relations between strata are non-antagonistic, being based on the division of labour.[24]

The contention that the abolition of a particular legal form of the control of the means of production can eliminate antagonism from a society is not an invitation to but an evasion of argument. Since I have made this point elsewhere,[25] I do not wish to dwell on it here. All I would like to say is that there are Marxist texts which are rather well suited to lend authority to this kind of contention.

When Marx wrote about bourgeois society being the last antagonistic form of society and its dissolution as bringing to an end the prehistory of human societies, he had already worked out firm ideas about the kind of social order by which it was to be replaced. The kind of society which would be associated with human history (as opposed to prehistory) is described in vivid detail in *The German Ideology*. In this kind of society 'nobody has one exclusive sphere of activity but each can become accomplished in any branch he wishes;

[23] Raymond Aron, 'Two Definitions of Class' in A. Béteille (ed.), *Social Inequality*, Penguin, 1969, p. 70.
[24] Béteille, 'The Politics of "Non-Antagonistic" Strata', op. cit.
[25] Ibid.

society regulates the general production and thus makes it possible
for me to do one thing today and another tomorrow, to hunt in the
morning, fish in the afternoon, rear cattle in the evening, criticise after
dinner, just as I have a mind, without ever becoming hunter, fisher-
man, shepherd or critic.'[26] I do not think that even the most ardent
Marxist in India would say today that this kind of society exists or is
being created in the Soviet Union, although I am not sure that a few
of them may not believe this about China.

Whereas Soviet scholars maintain that in their country a society
based on classes has been replaced by one based on the division of
labour, Marx believed that the dissolution of bourgeois society would
lead to the abolition not only of classes but of the division of labour
itself. Here we enter perilous ground, for I do not think that this kind
of argument can be saved by even the most ingenious definition.

It is clear that for Marx the true source of inequality, exploitation
and conflict lay not simply in the system of classes but in the division
of labour and, ultimately, in the very fact of labour. Hence it was
logical for him to believe that the only way to eliminate conflict,
exploitation and inequality was to abolish labour itself. 'The transformation, through the division of labour, of personal powers (relationships) into material powers, cannot be dispelled by dismissing
the general idea of it from one's mind, but can only be abolished by
the individuals again subjecting these material powers to themselves
and abolishing the division of labour.'[27] And further, 'Labour *is* free
in all civilized countries; it is not a matter of freeing labour but of
abolishing it.'[28]

Now, one can certainly believe that there will be a society in the
future where there will be no classes and no division of labour, and
where labour itself will cease to exist. But in the cold light of sociological reasoning this kind of belief is no different from the belief in
a life after death: it can be neither proved nor disproved.

It will be a mistake to dismiss the idea of a classless society freed
from the division of labour as merely a harmless fantasy. For there
are people who believe in it and their belief has important consequences for what they do, what they say and what they write.

Whereas Marx believed that the classless society would come into
being in the future, Marxists in our time believe that such a society,
or a close approximation to it already exists. Now, sociology as an

[26] Marx and Engels, *The German Ideology*, op. cit., p. 45.
[27] Ibid., p. 93.   [28] Ibid., p. 224.

intellectual discipline must be either fully comparative or nothing, which means that it must view every type of human society with the same critical detachment. This must in the end bring the sociologist into conflict with those who have a jealous attachment to some particular society, whether their own or another.

For thirty years Indian Marxists have had a jealous attachment to the Soviet Union. Soviet society embodied for them the virtues of humanism, justice and scientific progress. In it the worker had at last attained his true worth and dignity, was no longer anyone's inferior, and was free to conduct his life in accordance with principles that were at once humane and scientific. Committed Marxists in India did not doubt the truth of this because they had a theory which predicted the emergence of such a society after the working class Revolution. If they had any doubts they shared them only with others like themselves. To express such doubts in public was to cease to be a committed Marxist, and to become a Trotskyist—or something worse.

Indian Marxists, particularly of the younger generation, have no longer the same attachment to Soviet society. Some of them would go as far as to characterize its system as 'social imperialism'. It is ironic that the attachment to Soviet society should begin to weaken among men of goodwill at precisely that point of time when the Soviet leaders sought to free it from the yoke of Stalinism. All kinds of facts—which the sceptics had always suspected to be there—were brought out after 1956 to show how the old leadership had betrayed the Revolution. Several factors have been responsible for the disenchantment with Soviet society, but the most important of these, at least among younger Marxists in India, is the emergence of a more romantic alternative in China.

Students of human history and human psychology will have to explain how people who have been so rudely disillusioned once can so soon afterwards construct another illusion which is essentially so much like the first. I do not wish to comment on contemporary Chinese society about which very little is known. But one does not need to know very much about it in order to understand the Marxist attitude to China which is not very different from the earlier attitude towards the Soviet Union about which we do know a few things.

I think it would be no less foolish to cover Soviet or Chinese society with tar and feather than to believe that they embody higher virtues than other human societies have ever attained. The sociologist only demands that all societies—American, British, Chinese, Soviet as well as Indian—be viewed in the same cold, clear light. Marxists have done very well in exposing the inner contradictions of British imperialism, American capitalism and even Indian feudalism, but they have always treated one society—whether Soviet of Chinese—as a privileged exception. Sociology insists on treating all societies alike; it recognizes no privileged exceptions.

Index